THE POLITICS OF
PEACE-MAINTENANCE

THE POLITICS OF PEACE-MAINTENANCE

edited by
Jarat Chopra

foreword by
Chester A. Crocker

LYNNE
RIENNER
PUBLISHERS

BOULDER
LONDON

Published in the United States of America in 1998 by
Lynne Rienner Publishers, Inc.
1800 30th Street, Boulder, Colorado 80301

and in the United Kingdom by
Lynne Rienner Publishers, Inc.
3 Henrietta Street, Covent Garden, London WC2E 8LU

Chapters 1 through 7 of this book also appear as a special issue
of *Global Governance* (Volume 4, Number 1, Jan.–Mar. 1998).

Library of Congress Cataloging-in-Publication Data
The politics of peace-maintenance / edited by Jarat Chopra.
  Includes bibliographical references and index.
  ISBN 1-55587-756-7 (alk. paper)
  ISBN 1-55587-757-5 (pbk. : alk. paper)
  1. International police. 2. United Nations—Armed Forces.
1. Chopra, Jarat.
JZ6374.P65   1998
341.5'84—dc21   98-6172
                                                                            CIP

British Cataloguing in Publication Data
A Cataloguing in Publication record for this book
is available from the British Library.

Printed and bound in the United States of America

⊗   The paper used in this publication meets the requirements
     of the American National Standard for Permanence of
     Paper for Printed Library Materials Z39.48-1984.

5 4 3 2 1

To C.

In memoriam

Contents

Foreword
  Chester A. Crocker   ix

1 Introducing Peace-Maintenance   1
     Jarat Chopra

2 Establishing Political Authority in Peace-Maintenance   19
     W. Andy Knight

3 Organizing Civil Administration in Peace-Maintenance   41
     Sally Morphet

4 Reestablishing Law and Order in Peace-Maintenance   61
     Mark Plunkett

5 Asserting Humanitarianism in Peace-Maintenance   81
     Antonio Donini

6 Providing Military Security in Peace-Maintenance   97
     Richard P. Cousens

7 Accepting External Authority in Peace-Maintenance   107
     Clement E. Adibe

8 Critiquing Peace-Maintenance   123
     Duane Bratt

   Acronyms   135
   Index   137
   About the Book   145

Foreword

Chester A. Crocker

This volume raises the quality of the debate about humanitarian intervention and military operations other than war. It does so by incorporating trenchant lessons learned from the cases of the 1990s and by insisting on the overarching importance of strategic concepts that spell the difference between effective international action and failures or lost opportunities. In the process, the chapters that follow lay to rest some of the early half-truths and politically convenient judgments that emerged from our experience in such places as Bosnia, Rwanda, and Somalia. The historical record of multilateral intervention is set in a context that clearly documents the entire range of actions of which the international community has already demonstrated it is capable. The authors thereby illustrate the possibility of an evolution toward "best practices," and they enrich our conceptual tools for understanding what we are already doing (or not doing).

Editor Jarat Chopra sparked a lively debate with the introduction in 1995 of the term *peace-maintenance,* coined to distinguish the concept from both the largely diplomatic *peacekeeping* function between states and the largely military notions of *peace-enforcement* in situations of civil strife. Peace-maintenance, as developed further here, is proposed as a comprehensive political strategy for pulling together all forms of intervention and assistance that may be required when state institutions fail (or risk failing) and the "warlord syndrome" emerges.

Not everyone will be persuaded that such holistic strategic planning for intervention by leading actors in the international community is feasible or even desirable. Some will view these proposals as a call for unrestrained internationalism delinked from considerations of national interest and finite power resources. Others will point out the sweeping authority and responsibility that outsiders are expected to exercise in the affairs of people who have temporarily become victim to the breakdown or fragility of their own institutions. The sovereignty-supranationalism (not to mention "assertive multilateralism") debates are seldom absent from these discussions.

Still others will point out that while peace-maintenance might be possible in an ideal world, there are many alternative priorities to consume our energy and attention, resource constraints at a time of shrinking militaries and disaster fatigue, and an uncertain stock of political will without which creative strategic action is doomed. Some may even wonder if the peace-maintenance terminology helps advance the frontiers of conceptual clarity when many sweeping phrases linked to peace have been given a bad name by the recent performance of what we choose to call the international community.

But this book contains practical guidance as well as bold strategic proposals. The authors accept as givens the hard lessons we face about (1) the impossibility of politically "neutral" humanitarian intervention; (2) the likelihood of perverse and unintended consequences when humanitarian action occurs in a political-military vacuum; (3) the demonstrated shortcomings of many recent experiments in multilateral intervention management by the UN and other agencies; (4) the predictable failures that flow from action that is motivated by the need to be seen to be "doing something" and by time-defined exit strategies; and (5) the lively prospect of failure when external action is divorced from local political alliances and does not generate internal political legitimacy—a likelihood enhanced by a narrow focus on holding elections in polities that are both polarized and militarized.

It is on the basis of this knowledge that the book develops its case for peace-maintenance, encompassing scenarios ranging from *governorship* to less intrusive forms of political action such as selective *control, partnership* with local authority, and *assistance* to government offices. The chapters discuss the full gamut of functional tasks (establishing transitional political authority, conducting civil administration, maintaining law and order with justice, delivering humanitarian assistance, providing military security, and linking external decisionmakers with the local politics of legitimacy). At the same time, they encompass most of the modern cases of operations other than war in all the regions where civil chaos occurs.

To this observer, the most compelling argument here is about the necessity for comprehensive thinking and coherence (or unity) of action. For too long, it has been trendy to assert that specialists in different disciplines need to be relatively unburdened by each other's baggage and subjected only to the loosest forms of coordination in national capitals or the field. Similarly, the bureaucratic fudge factories of the UN system and the dilemmas of military-humanitarian (to say nothing of military-to-military) coordination are often cited as reasons for accepting that interventionism must be disorderly. In turn, this "fact" is used to justify scaling back the global response to civil chaos.

But these arguments are cop-outs. It is not written on stone tablets that we cannot learn from mistakes, that complex operations must fail, or that inept or inappropriate personnel will always be placed in charge of interventions. For all their inadequacies, the North Atlantic Treaty Organization

and Organization for Security and Co-operation in Europe have demonstrated in Bosnia that incremental learning is possible. The United States
and UN in Haiti have also shown a capacity for learning. The critical
lessons from these and other places, such as Mozambique and Namibia, include: the importance of political commitment and staying power; the need
for a comprehensive framework of action linked to an operational center of
gravity and a critical mass of resources; the demand for clearly defined
goals about the "end state" (or definition of success); and the imperative of
unity of field level operational authority and military command.

None of the concepts and suggestions in the book will be properly implemented without broader public debate and understanding. It is unrea-
sonable to expect political leaders simply to impose on their media-
drenched electorates a full-blown vision of these recommendations for
improved management of their national and global security. At the same
time, these pages offer some basis for believing that political courage may
have its reward. ⊕

Note

Chester A. Crocker is research professor in the practice of diplomacy at George-
town University and chairman of the board, U.S. Institute of Peace. He was formerly U.S. assistant secretary of state for African affairs.

1

Introducing Peace-Maintenance

———————— ⊕ ————————

Jarat Chopra

"Seek ye first the political kingdom and all other things shall be added unto you." So proclaimed Ghanaian leader Kwame Nkrumah in the 1950s regarding the critical ingredient of African independence. Despite the perils of promises, the same may be said today of an international community contending with unprecedented social transformations. The dramatic, painful, and often violent pulses of change, inevitably, have not fitted within the boundaries of states or strictures of sovereignty.[1] Neither lengthy evolutions nor quick revolutions can be managed by polite, long-distance diplomacy or military force alone, or without vision and controlled direction. The ability to steer events rests in the political realm. However, UN member states have sought first to offer development or deliver humanitarian assistance. Consequently, food and aid have been consumed more by competing factions than by victim populations, and converted into a simple but devastating kind of weaponry in Somalia, Rwanda, and Zaire.

We have been at war. We now understand this to have been true, statistically. The five years between 1990 and 1995 proved to be twice as lethal as any half decade since the end of World War II. According to avowedly conservative estimates, there were ninety-three wars involving seventy countries. Of the 22 million people who perished in armed conflict since 1945, 5.5 million of them, some one quarter, died in the early 1990s. Furthermore, war has ceased to be primarily a profession of arms: if at the beginning of the twentieth century 85–90 percent of war deaths were soldiers, by the end, on average, 75 percent are civilians—and the figure is considerably higher in some estimates.[2] The current character of interstate relations, conditioned by the grand diplomacy of the Cold War, could not avert the internecine killing by peoples redefining themselves and their positions globally.

It is as if the organizational pattern established by the political competition of the last great war fifty years ago is now being challenged, perhaps almost unconsciously—more as the natural result of social imperatives not accommodated by that pattern than by virtue of some new and compelling ideology. And even the limited response of the Security Council is no less profound. The year 1992 may turn out to have been revolutionary—a kind of 1917 or 1789—for the UN. Member states conducted perhaps the greatest experiments in international organization since the drafting and signing of the UN Charter. That is, the largest and most complex operations in UN history were deployed that year simultaneously to Cambodia, Somalia, and the former Yugoslavia, to stop wars and to secure a degree of well-being for local populations.

While significant, the diplomatic and military limitations of these and other vast efforts in internal conflicts indicated that social competition necessitated political management. Already, the static diplomatic character of traditional, inter-state peacekeeping had burst its bounds in a hot peace after a cold war, and the use of military force was called on to fill the gap in what became the so-called second generation of UN peace operations.[3] This period witnessed the reemergence of the term *peace-enforcement.* In the years immediately before and after the signing of the UN Charter, peace-enforcement was virtually synonymous with the idea of collective security, in which military force was authorized jointly and employed by powerful states to prevent and halt acts of aggression. It referred to what has come to be known simply as "enforcement," of the kind envisioned in Article 42 of Chapter VII of the charter.

However, after four decades of "peacekeeping"—a word that neither appears in the charter nor was uttered during the period of its formulation—other "peace" terms gained currency that fitted more in the context of distinguishing lower level operational categories and doctrine than referred explicitly to the existing model of international organization. So "peace-enforcement" was used by then UN Secretary-General Boutros Boutros-Ghali in *An Agenda for Peace* to describe what had been already identified as a middle ground in the use of force, between defensive peacekeeping and high-intensity enforcement. This "third option" was not synonymous with the kinds of total war that might be necessitated in the suppression of aggression.

In the juridical history of Article 1(1) of the UN Charter, which refers to collective measures for the maintenance of international peace and security, the term *peace-maintenance* is referred to intermittently between the Atlantic Charter in 1942 and the drafters conference in San Francisco three years later. The principal planners, including particularly Franklin D. Roosevelt,[4] attempted to express the scope and purpose of a novel form of permanent organization in the postwar world. It was not the passive preservation of a diplomatic status quo but the active determination of law and order internationally, in the manner of a domestic political community. Peace was not to be elusive and only occasionally kept, but convincingly and perpetually "maintained." The extent of earlier proposals was narrowed first by the wartime agreements of the United States, Britain, and the Soviet Union; second, by the opinions of smaller powers; and finally, by great-power geopolitical competition. But the remaining political kernel defined the "collective" character and separate legal personality of the UN, and distinguished it from the merely "cooperative" nature of the League of Nations.

Now, after the Cold War, in the midst of new conflagrations, and after conditioning by decades of peacekeeping and years of second-generation experiments with the use of force, the term *peace-maintenance* is reborn as a "unified concept" for peace missions. This chapter—which introduces a book first published as a special issue of the journal *Global Governance*—distinguishes diplomatic peacekeeping and military peace-enforcement from political peace-maintenance. It also provides a context for the succeeding chapters, each of which explores a separate component of peace-maintenance. W. Andy Knight discusses how such operations establish political authority. In her analysis, Sally Morphet focuses on the organization of civil administration. Mark Plunkett examines the reestablishment of law and order. Antonio Donini outlines the challenges of asserting humanitarianism, while Richard P. Cousens reviews those of providing military security. Clement E. Adibe describes the conditions under which local populations may accept external authority. And finally, Duane Bratt's conclusion critiques the preceding chapters and considers the future of politics of peace-maintenance. Together, the authors recognize the need for a globally effective political capability, and their arguments reflect that the evolution of peace operations doctrine has entered a third and, perhaps, final phase.

Diplomatic Peacekeeping and Military Peace-Enforcement

The first phase of peace operations doctrine, the era of traditional "peacekeeping," lasted from 1948 to 1989, during which some fifteen operations were deployed.[5] This Cold War period was characterized by diplomatic frameworks, the result of what conventional UN parlance referred to as "peace-making." As a consequence of diplomacy, limited military forces and civilian personnel were deployed symbolically to guarantee negotiated settlements, invariably between two sovereign states. This practice developed certain basic assumptions:[6]

1. A force had to operate with the full confidence and backing of the Security Council.
2. A force operated only with the full consent and cooperation of the parties in conflict.
3. Command and control of the force would be vested in the secretary-general and the force commander, under the authority of the Security Council.

4. The composition of the force would represent a wide geographic spectrum, although conventionally excluding the permanent members of the Security Council, and contingents would be supplied voluntarily by member states upon the secretary-general's request.
5. Armed force would be used only in self-defense, although self-defense included defense of the mandate as well as the peacekeeper.
6. The force would operate with complete impartiality.

Observers in blue berets or peacekeepers in blue helmets supervised clear lines separating belligerents in places as diverse as the Golan Heights between Israel and Syria; Kashmir between India and Pakistan; and Nicosia between Greek and Turkish communities in Cyprus. The UN's mission to Lebanon in 1978—the last peacekeeping operation for nearly a decade—was deployed in the midst of factional militia manipulated by neighboring governments in Syria and Israel, and foreshadowed the future landscape of UN catastrophes. A turning point occurred in 1989 when a decolonization mission arrived in Namibia, mandated with a wider range of tasks than were authorized for previous verification observers or interposition forces.[7]

Traditional peacekeeping principles were necessarily challenged. In particular, consent of the parties in conflict was not always forthcoming or was sometimes withdrawn once given. In response, UN operations would have to consider using force. This would require sufficient assets to do so and the inclusion in operations of armed forces from Security Council permanent members. In turn, the issue of command and control of assets would become more acute. Impartiality would be defined as the objectivity with which the mandate was executed rather than the degree of submission to the will of the parties in conflict. This would give the Security Council an even more crucial role in developing clear instructions, continually supporting the force in the field with the solidarity of its will, and expanding mandates as changes in ground conditions required. These new requirements reflected that a second generation of operations had come into being, beyond symbolic peacekeeping but short of Gulf War–style enforcement.

In this next phase, specifically between 1989 and 1994, some eighteen operations were deployed, more than had been dispatched in the UN's first forty-five years. The challenging environment of internal conflicts necessitated the development of a concept for the limited and gradually escalating use of armed force for multinational missions. UN military operations could be divided into nine categories, arranged in three levels of varying degrees of force. At one extreme were level one operations: the familiar tasks of observer missions and peacekeeping forces. At the other end of the spectrum were the level three tasks of sanctions and high-intensity operations, which are characteristic of Articles 41 and 42, respectively, of the

UN Charter. The five level two tasks in between represented the latest doctrinal developments, as follows:[8]

1. *Preventive deployment*: A UN force may be deployed to an area where tension is rising between two parties, to avoid the outbreak of hostilities or the maturing of an existing conflict. This area may be between two states or between two factions within a state. Examples include the UN Preventive Deployment Force (UNPREDEP) in Macedonia and the UN Iraq-Kuwait Observation Mission (UNIKOM), a trigger mechanism between Gulf War adversaries.

2. *Internal conflict resolution measures*: A UN force may be required to underwrite a multiparty cease-fire within a state. It may have to demobilize and canton warring factions, secure their weapons, and stabilize the theater of conflict. UN operations in Cambodia and Mozambique illustrated this type of activity.

3. *Assistance to interim civil authorities*: A UN force may be required to underwrite a transition process and transfer of power in a country reestablishing its civil society from the ashes of conflict. It may have to provide security during *(a)* the repatriation of refugees, *(b)* the organization and conduct of elections, and *(c)* the early stages of infrastructure rehabilitation. This series of tasks was essential in transition operations in Namibia, Cambodia, and El Salvador.

4. *Protection of humanitarian relief operations*: A UN force may be deployed to establish a mounting base, a delivery site, and a corridor between the two to protect the provision and distribution of humanitarian relief by UN and nongovernmental civilian agencies. This activity met with varying degrees of success in Somalia, Bosnia, Rwanda, and northern Iraq.

5. *Guarantee and denial of movement*: A UN force may be called on to secure the rights of passage in international waterways and airspace, or across national territory. A force may also be required to restrict movement of parties designated as delinquent by the international community. Examples include the efforts in Bosnia and in northern and southern Iraq.

In reference to this middle ground in the use of force, Boutros-Ghali included the term *peace-enforcement* in *An Agenda for Peace*. However, after the UN was militarily routed in places such as Somalia,[9] he reverted to the black-and-white options of defensive peacekeeping and high-intensity enforcement, relegating peace-enforcement back to the latter and equating it again with action of the type outlined in Article 42.[10] This reaction was impractical to sustain, and at a press conference only two days after issuing the "Supplement to An Agenda for Peace," the secretary-general had to distinguish between peace-enforcement and "huge peace enforcement operations."[11] Meanwhile, in national departments and ministries of defense, such as in the U.K., the term *peace support* has been used to refer to the variety of military tasks undertaken in multifunctional missions. While the underlying doctrine indicates support of a framework, it does not identify the nature of that framework.

Also, a misnomer emerged, "second generation peacekeeping."[12] It confused the narrowly defined practice of peacekeeping, on the one hand, and, on the other, second-generation operations that were not exclusively reliant on consent of belligerents and that did not restrict the use of force to self-defense alone. Precisely the application of a diplomatic peacekeeping approach in challenging environments proved fatal in Cambodia, Angola, and the former Yugoslavia, and in most other operations as well.

Furthermore, the artificiality of a "third generation" of peace operations has exacerbated the confusion. When Boutros-Ghali first acknowledged the emergence of a second generation, he also suggested the existence—simultaneously, and rather illogically, therefore—of a third generation, defined by institutional "peace-building."[13] These concepts have since become more distorted by a reversal of their meanings: second-generation operations have been defined as consensual peace-building, and third-generation operations as peace-enforcement equated with high-intensity enforcement.[14]

The complex, multifunctional operations of the second phase, designed to supervise transitions from conditions of social conflict to minimal political order, had limited impact because of excessive reliance on either diplomatic peacekeeping or military peace-enforcement. Consequently, transitional arrangements required but did not achieve better coordination between military forces, humanitarian assistance, and civilian components organizing elections, protecting human rights, or conducting administrative and executive tasks of government. In *An Agenda for Peace*, "post-conflict peace-building" referred to longer-term development, strengthening institutions, and fostering conditions that could vitiate violence as a means of political competition. But this kind of "assistance" is incapable of either ensuring accountability of an oppressive regime or reconstituting fragmented authority. Another concept has been needed.

Political Peace-Maintenance

On the ground, the UN has had to contend with the contradictory phenomena of too much order and authority by a powerful government, such as in El Salvador or Namibia, and of varying degrees of anarchy, as in Cambodia and Somalia. In the incoherent malaise of factionalism, a kind of "warlord syndrome" emerged in which the appetites of power could mobilize religion in Lebanon, ethnicity in the former Yugoslavia, and relatively homogeneous clan lineages in Somalia. Unchecked by either a weakened population below or the diluted resolve of the international community above, factional leaders proliferated and inherited the places where UN deployments proved ineffective. Interstate diplomacy conducted by institution-reliant bureaucrats between factional leaders in internal conflicts served to further fragment conditions of anarchy. Use of military force without sufficiently clear political objectives led inevitably to confrontation. Commanders reacted to the imperatives of combat, including defeat of an enemy, rather than creating conditions that could be supported and sustained in the long term.

The current third phase of peace operations doctrine needs to elaborate functional dimensions of a political framework. Despite the danger of adding yet another debased "peace" term to a prevalent kind of "bluespeak"—and not as the result of the desire to coin a new phrase, but as a natural reconsideration of the essential basis of the UN Charter—the goal of "peace-maintenance" can be associated with this third phase. The term *peace-maintenance* must be used in its intended sense.[15] Specifically, it refers to the overall political framework, as part of which the objectives of diplomatic activities, humanitarian assistance, military forces, and civilian components are not only coordinated but harmonized. The concept provides a link between the strategic and operational levels of command and control, and constitutes the exercise by the international community as a whole of political authority within nations.

The UN tends to confuse the terms *diplomatic* and *political*. In Clausewitzian fashion, former U.S. secretary of state James Baker argued that "diplomacy *is* the continuation of politics."[16] This would imply that the two are related but not synonymous. Yet the UN refers to the "political process" as the attempt to reach a degree of reconciliation between factions or states. The process is considered "political" not just because it addresses the conclusion of a long-term settlement between states or the establishment of a unified executive authority internally. But calling it "political" also distinguishes it from other components of an operation— military security, humanitarian assistance, or electoral organization, for instance. However, in such "political processes," the UN behaves as a diplomat and interlocutor, a representative of an authority far away, but fails to exercise executive powers itself.

Diplomacy may be a logical practice to pursue when separating two states, since each one has a government with political authority. In the no-man's-land in between, the UN need not come to terms with its jurisdiction over an area, or with its relationship to territory, the local population, or executive authority. It need be concerned only with the limited locations of its deployments and the placement of troops and armaments of the belligerents, since the government of each state is still juridically responsible for a portion of the buffer zone up to the international boundary, even if the exact position of that boundary is in dispute.

Within a state, however, reliance on diplomacy is not tenable. The UN cannot remain aloof of its relationship to territory or to the local population over which it may have claimed jurisdiction, and therefore must recognize its role in the exercise of executive political authority. It may have to fulfill this role independently in anarchical conditions, or jointly with an existing regime. Even in the latter case, if the UN is to effectively ensure accountability, it needs an independent political decisionmaking capability, as well as law and order institutions available at its disposal. In both cases, the UN would be defeating its own efforts if it were at the same time to depend on local authority structures (whether coherent and oppressive or fragmented and negligible) and attempt to reconstitute a new authority.

In fact, doing so draws the mission into the existing conditions of local authority, as the UN gravitates toward what it is permitted to do by a regime or warlords. The mission either becomes beholden to the will of a powerful government or is undermined by factionalism in anarchical conditions. In Western Sahara and El Salvador, the UN strengthened the hand of the stronger: of Morocco and the government in San Salvador, respectively. In Cambodia, it joined the Cambodians' competition for control of Phnom Penh, which for centuries never implied control of the rest of the country. In Somalia, its loosely arranged coalition fragmented due to the irresistible forces of anarchy when UN commanders proved incapable of replacing U.S. leadership.

To avoid being undermined, the UN must deploy decisively and establish a center of gravity around which local individuals and institutions can coalesce until a new authority structure is established and transferred to a legitimately determined, indigenous leadership. In the interim period, the UN needs to counterbalance or even displace the oppressor or warlords. This implies that the UN claims jurisdiction over the entire territory and ought to deploy throughout if it can. It establishes a direct relationship with the local people who will eventually participate in the reconstitution of authority and inherit the newly established institutions.

This is the meaning of a political framework, an overall blue umbrella, under which law and order are maintained once a UN center and periphery are delineated. It is distinct from the notion of intervention as part of interstate relations, in which entry into an area is only partial and territory is incidental to limited objectives. Authority cannot be exercised based on a perceptual axis of inside, outside, and between, as is the essence of diplomacy. A political framework is all-pervasive and connected to the total social process locally. It links that domestic population with an international mandate as the basis of authority, in defiance of malevolent institutions of belligerents. Like the purpose of a rule of law, peace-maintenance must be a means of transforming the position of the weak as against the strong; it is an outside guarantor of a kind of internal self-determination.

Could the UN possibly do this? In the manner that it commands and controls fully integrated operations, the answer is likely no. During the second phase, at times the UN had to assume executive political powers on paper; but in the field, with a peacekeeping mandate, it exercised its authority diplomatically, through negotiation rather than independently. Consequently, the UN failed to control political institutions in Cambodia, was manipulated by Morocco in Western Sahara, and broke apart into the separate agendas of contributing contingents in Somalia.

If accountable and effective peace missions are to be deployed, then a mechanism for operational political direction and ongoing decisionmaking in the field needs to be devised. Collective mandates from the international community as a whole, as authorized by the Security Council or General Assembly, will be necessary for legality and legitimacy. However, to connect genuine collective accountability and effectiveness in the field, given the limitations (now legion) of the UN, a political directorate may include the UN as only one member, but would also include regional organizations; interested and disinterested member states—those with and without a stake in the outcome of the conflict, respectively; and local representatives who will have to assume ultimate control of the transitional authority. Depending on local conditions, the joint political mechanism may be established on the basis of consent of an existing authority or in the wake of military force pursuant to a collective determination if only competing factions are prevalent.

Ultimately, the critical factor for success or failure of peace-maintenance rests with the role of the local community, whom the effort is intended to help—as Antonio Donini and Clement Adibe emphasize in their chapters. Reliance on prejudicial local structures has proved mistaken, since the UN serves to affirm and not challenge the status quo. At the same time, warlords and factions are well armed facts and the power of existing regimes is self-evident. Therefore, they must be part of any equation, but they cannot be permitted to dominate an international authority. No authority, malevolent or benign, can survive without the balance of popular consent in its favor. Successful peace-maintenance is premised on this fact. Therefore the role local representatives play in a joint authority will have to be determined according to the specifics of the case.

Peace-maintenance is not some colonial enterprise. While there are generic principles that can be learned regarding the administration of territory and population from any model of governance, the purpose and behavior of peace-maintenance is opposite to colonialism, and, in fact, it can be a means of decolonization.[17] Colonial domination is a unilateral enterprise; a joint interim authority is a collectively accountable body. In the past, the difference between a colony and a trust territory may have been limited, with a variation, perhaps, in the manner of policing the two. The peace-maintenance project, however, is rooted in another context, tackles another set of tasks, and is motivated by another dimension of imperatives. While a colonial power draws resources from a colony, an international authority directs resources into a nation. A colonial power plays the role of master, and the colonized, the servant. But in peace-maintenance, the international authority is the servant of both an international and locally supported rule of law and order.[18]

The goal of peace-maintenance is not imposition of an alien system or a preconceived style of operation functioning in a social vacuum. The need for a local international authority is precisely to create a flexible decisionmaking capability that can respond to local needs with political, anthropological, and sociological sensitivity. While generic facets of peace-maintenance can be identified, their implementation needs to be locally responsive and directed on an ongoing basis. In the same manner that the second generation of UN operations required an expansion of traditional peacekeeping principles into a wider doctrine, so too the current phase requires a doctrine for a political framework and the variety of civilian tasks associated with it.

Operational Peace-Maintenance

There is a fracture between the political legitimacy of decisions made by the international community as a whole and the effectiveness of operations implementing these decisions. On the one hand, this has led to the questionable accountability of states implementing UN decisions, such as the widely criticized, disproportionate response of the United States to Iraqi aggression in Kuwait.[19] On the other, it has led to legitimate but ineffective UN operations, as in Angola and the former Yugoslavia. Peace agreements brokered by UN diplomats could not be translated into action because operational considerations had not been adequately assessed, and either the Secretariat did not have the means or the capability to implement increasingly challenging mandates issued by the Security Council or it was practically not possible to fulfill the military and civilian tasks in the field assumed diplomatically in New York.

Political Authority

Given diminished consent of parties in the field and eroded support of a tired international community to the level of commitment required by UN operations, there is need to fill the void of the missing link, as Andy Knight argues in the next chapter. A cell composed of the parties, the UN, and key member states is one way to generate political will on a continuous basis not only to conclude peace agreements initially, but to interpret these on an agreed basis, and perhaps even to implement them through a joint presence in the field. This should reduce reliance on peace-enforcement, which can be reserved for specific tasks as part of a well integrated political strategy. It would also enable states limiting their participation at the UN to remain engaged in a cost-effective or politically sustainable manner and could in fact lead as a catalyst to greater commitment to success in the field.

Something of an indirect analogy may be drawn from the Joint Monitoring Commission (JMC) that supervised the decolonization of Namibia. It was composed of Angola, Cuba, and South Africa, with the United States and Soviet Union as active observers. The JMC helped develop consensus and a peace agreement initially, and it played a significant role when the process nearly derailed.[20]

The variable factors affecting the United Nations Transition Assistance Group (UNTAG) in Namibia are not directly comparable to other missions. Nevertheless, the JMC was of general significance as a kind of "court of appeal" that met regularly and could call emergency sessions to discuss all political and military aspects of implementation of agreements made. There was also a Joint Military Monitoring Commission (JMMC) composed of the same military powers and responsible to the political JMC. As a link between the diplomatic, military, and political aspects of the operation, the JMC could fill gaps in negotiated agreements and ensure common interpretation of provisions.

It provided *confidence* and *leverage* in the process. The parties could not be relied on exclusively to keep the process on track; at the same time, it was their process and only they could ensure success. The UN as a court of appeal was not adequate and one goal of the JMC was to keep the United States and Soviet Union continuously engaged. Two UNTAG officials, UN Special Representative Martti Ahtisaari and Force Commander Lt. Gen. Prem Chand, participated as "expert observers." The JMC could have become a proto-regional organization but it did not; and its impact should not be overestimated, since a large number of factors contributed to overall success in the field, including the historical role of Namibia on the international agenda, the years of preparation before implementation, and the special representative's diplomatic acumen.

Russia has employed a similar mechanism in its "peace-creation" operations in the "near abroad" conflicts of the former Soviet Union.[21] The end of the Cold War meant a redefinition of mission and restructuring of forces for both Moscow's Ministry of Defense and the U.S. Pentagon. This included the need: to respond to a different scope of low-intensity operations; to experiment with peacekeeping, in which neither conventionally had participated; and to shift from preparing for mass-scale war. But by virtue of necessity, Russian forces have had to develop more radically new instruments than has the United States for the challenges they face not far away but close to home. They have resorted to the evolution of peace-keeping-plus operations and applied a unique variation of this in the newly independent republics, which in turn has developed a sophisticated mechanism for peace-maintenance.

Russian operations in the near abroad are securing specifically Moscow's interests, whether of the Ministry of Defense, of President Boris Yeltsin, or in some cases of the general in the field. However, delete Russian interests and insert genuinely international interests and the result is a valuable model and set of lessons for UN operations. Developing limited use of force strategies and tactics, much as European powers did during their colonial run-down, is not the reason for the effectiveness of Russian operations. It is, rather, the sensitivity with which military forces and political goals are orchestrated among both high- and low-ranking officers in the field, perhaps partly as a result of the historically political culture of the Soviet military. Also, Russians are well acquainted with the areas and players where they operate, unlike the UN; and unlike the tendency of the UN, the Russians take full advantage of this fact.

The mechanism that coordinates political goals and military forces is a Joint Control Commission (JCC). It has developed gradually, and where it was not used, as in Tajikistan, the imperatives of combat proceeded uncontrollably. In Moldova, the JCC was composed of the two parties, Moldova and the puppet regime of the Dniester Republic, with Russia as a big brother and first among equals. The Conference, now Organization, on Security and Cooperation in Europe (OSCE) was supposed to be an observer to ensure its impartiality, but was only permitted access to the body after several years. Responsible to the JCC was a separation of forces "peacekeeping" mission; with checkpoints in a buffer zone guarded by Russia and the belligerents themselves. Russia provided heavy armaments and therefore the "peace-enforcement" element of the mission. There were also "observers" responsible to the JCC that monitored the checkpoints. The nearby Fourteenth Army, formerly commanded by the formidable Gen. Aleksandr Lebed, provided a deterrent capability and ensured a cease-fire that has held since its inception.

However, the JCC in Moldova was not impartial and it proved to be an effective means by which Russia could manipulate the parties to suit its interests. Nevertheless, an accountable form of this could be a means of controlling recalcitrant warlords, whose participation is necessary in a peace process, and who have managed successfully to challenge the international law and authority of the UN. A similar mechanism is pending in South Ossetia with the full participation of the OSCE, but it is yet to be realized. Most significantly in the proposal for the first genuinely joint international-Russian mission to Nagorno-Karabakh, OSCE observers were to be deployed throughout key posts of the Russian forces, which were to be responsible to a JCC-like framework under OSCE chairmanship. This provided an example of a realistic and flexible mechanism worth considering given limited international resources, overall fatigue, and the need to provide accountability for great-power action. A similar experiment to note was the deployment of U.S. "liaison" personnel with Russian units participating in the Implementation Force (IFOR) in Bosnia.

These designs can be distinguished from the situation in Abkhazia. UN military observers deployed in a separate mission, but loosely cooperating with Russian forces, did not gain adequate access to Russian decisionmaking. The overall diplomatic framework for negotiations in Geneva under UN chairmanship, furthermore, could not provide the kind of confidence and leverage that was required for accountability in the field.

The Nagorno-Karabakh proposal also was unlike the model in Cambodia in which a Supreme National Council (SNC) composed of the warring factions did not include the UN in an integrated manner and led to confrontation rather than combined action. The absence of a joint mechanism between the factions and the UN at the operational level meant that each administrative issue that arose assumed political proportions and led to the UN negotiating rather than exercising its wide powers. Such an operational mechanism apparently had been envisioned by the UN negotiator of the peace plans, Rafeeuddin Ahmed; but he was replaced just before deployment of the operation by Yasushi Akashi as special representative of the secretary-general, and this led to the loss of the unwritten understanding, the fracturing of the SNC at the political level, and the overall dysfunction of the operation.

Operational Categories

A UN political directorate may be deployed in one of several transitional scenarios. The UN might assume exclusive responsibility in an area and administer as a governor-in-trust, or it may participate in some joint arrangement in which it assumes responsibilities of a transition phase but does not physically conduct all the tasks of governance. In the latter case, it would exercise varying degrees of authority and either control local authority, enter into a partnership with it, or render it assistance:

1. *Governorship:* The UN assumes full responsibilities for conducting the affairs of government. This may occur when there is a total collapse of local state structures or where the state structures were imposed by a colonial or occupying power that has withdrawn. The UN may assume the tasks of governance itself and deploy a specific operation for the purpose or it may assume these responsibilities in name and appoint a single power or group of powers as agents to perform tasks on its behalf. This would require some mechanism of effective accountability that would ensure continued direction by the UN of the powers conducting the operation.

2. *Control:* An operation deployed to the area in question may have

been authorized under a mandate to exercise the powers of "direct control." In this event, the UN authority in the field would deploy throughout the instruments of the state or administering authority—including ministries, the judicial system, and police and armed forces. Once deployed, UN observers would monitor the local authority conducting the affairs of state. In the event that local officials commit an infraction according to the terms of the overall mandate of the transition process, the UN has the overriding authority to "take corrective action" by dismissing personnel or redirecting a local policy decision.

3. *Partnership:* The local authority may be powerful and may have adequate resources, because it is a colonial power repatriating, an occupation force withdrawing, or a totalitarian regime submitting itself to a democratizing process. In this case, the UN authority-in-trust may behave more as a partner of the local authority, given the coherent structures of governance in place. Being at least an equal in the joint authority, the UN would have a veto power in decision-making and a final say in the transition period. With the robust support of the Security Council or committed engagement of outside powers, the UN may achieve a status of "first among equals."

4. *Assistance:* The local administration may not be in complete disarray and the trust authority provides some overall coherence and an international standard for the development of government structures. Local structures in place may have been mishandled or abused, spawned an opposition, and constituted a source of conflict. The trust authority behaves as an independent advisor, identifying flaws in the local system and suggesting corrections.

In each case, according to Sally Morphet, the UN may intend to organize and conduct or supervise an election in order to transfer power from one authority to another. In the interim period, the UN may have assumed juridical authority over the area on paper, even if in the past it has rarely managed to do this physically. To be an authority in the area, a mission must accept the juridical implications of being in possession of power if it is to be in a position to transfer that power to a new authority. To do so, it must manage to physically wrest authority from an unaccountable regime or assume it and establish a center of gravity in the midst of anarchical conditions.

Furthermore, a joint authority may have to decide whether, anthropologically, an election is the correct means of establishing or transferring authority. In Cambodia and Somalia, for instance, factions did not share the UN perception that an election implied a winner, a loser, and a transfer of power; in both countries, voting figures were perceived as just one bargaining chip in a self-developing balance of power. The UN has treated elections as an exit strategy for itself more than elections have resulted in sustainable results. As such, they have been short-term responses to conditions requiring longer-term attention. Therefore, joint authority cannot be exclusively reliant on one-time votes as an end by themselves; they can be only one of a number of activities, all of which require each other as part of a single framework if order is to be sustainable.

In joint forms of civil administration, the powers of direct control or corrective action will have to be underwritten by an independent capacity to exercise the UN's will. While this may be selectively applied in instances where a flaw exists or an infraction has been committed, the operation will nevertheless need to have effective means of governance at its disposal. Described in more detail by Mark Plunkett, the elements of law and order include: UN civilian police forces; an independent means of criminal prosecution; and a criminal law developed for UN operations generally that takes account of human rights issues. Fostering a rule of law may be possible only in the context of a secure environment provided by the kinds of multinational military forces outlined by Richard Cousens. It needs to be combined with material and humanitarian assistance—not only so that order guarantees justice but also so that the population can experience a real difference in its daily life.

1. *Civilian police forces:* Unlike civilian police (CIVPOL) units in peacekeeping operations in Cyprus, Namibia, and even Cambodia, a police force capable of effectively enforcing law and order decisions of UN political authority will require a clear mandate with full policing powers of reporting, investigation, search, seizure, arrest, and detention. While local police forces should bear the brunt of law and order duties, with which CIVPOL may cooperate, the UN force must be able to conduct its tasks independently of the local police, particularly if the local forces refuse to enforce a decision of the joint authority or if the local police themselves violate the UN mandate in place. CIVPOL should be prepared not to underwrite but to challenge local law according to the UN law regulating the transition process. CIVPOL will require detention facilities to temporarily hold prisoners liable to prosecution, as well as to hold prisoners sentenced to longer-term imprisonment.

2. *Criminal prosecution*: The joint authority will require an independent process of prosecution. It will need a panel of judges, which may include local judges; but the UN cannot rely on the inconsistencies of local systems of prosecution, which may be dependent on an executive authority that is corrupt or ineffective. This independent mechanism should be available for both local offenders and members of the UN operation guilty of criminal activity. It must also be independent of the executive officers of the UN mission.

3. *Criminal law*: In addition to the overall mandate of the transition process, a specific criminal law needs to be developed for UN operations generally, applicable to both local and UN offenders. This should be a simplified document that takes account of various legal systems and likely will be limited in the first instance to blatant violations. Practice and application will create the larger body of law for this activity.

4. *Human rights:* While the criminal law may focus on basic crimes, such as murder and monetary corruption, special account should be taken of the unique dimensions of human rights law. Integration between domestically conceived criminal activity and human rights violations will have to be achieved.

Conclusion

Peace-maintenance as a "unified concept" for UN operations needs to integrate diplomatic, military, and humanitarian activities as part of an overall political strategy. The umbrella framework that coordinates these elements will need to be the UN administrator as politician if complex transitional arrangements in internal conflicts are to be successful. The tasks of political administration are ultimately the glue that maintains the coherence of a comprehensive strategy. If any of the diplomatic, military, or humanitarian aspects of operations dominates the others, an imbalance results from the vacuum of subordinated elements.

The UN to date has not adequately developed political strategies commensurate with diplomatic, military, and humanitarian activities. This has led to limited success in the field and, at times, to failure. The specifics of military operations and humanitarian assistance are being identified. A similar political exercise is required. The evolution of civil administration and the UN's political role in internal conflicts builds on the organization's experience and in joint form it will be more cost-effective than reliance on military peace-enforcement. At the same time, it provides a vehicle for the development of military capabilities in a palatable manner and for better administration of humanitarian activities.

If peace-maintenance is to be successfully developed then it must be collectively underwritten by the international community as a whole. Sovereignty and the barriers that the concept has raised cannot resist UN concern for issues that are deemed international, and the scope of "international" is widening to the point that collective political authority becomes a necessity rather than an infringement. However, the psychological shift among populations in the area of peace operations or on home fronts of nations contributing personnel have not kept pace with these global developments. The costs in the long term of not intervening will have to be understood as greater than those of intervening in the short term. Outlining the dimensions, implications, requirements, and evolution of peace-maintenance is a first step. ⊕

Notes

Jarat Chopra is research associate and lecturer in international law at the Thomas J. Watson Jr. Institute for International Studies at Brown University, and director of the institute's project on "Peace-Maintenance Operations." He was formerly assistant director of the Ford Foundation–funded research project on "Second Generation Multinational Forces" and special assistant in peacekeeping at the International Institute for Strategic Studies in London.

1. Jarat Chopra and Thomas G. Weiss, "Sovereignty is no Longer Sacrosanct: Codifying Humanitarian Intervention," *Ethics and International Affairs* 6 (1992): 95–117.

2. Dan Smith, "Towards Understanding the Causes of War," in Ketil Volden and Dan Smith, eds., *Causes of Conflict in the Third World* (Oslo: North/South Coalition and International Peace Research Institute, 1997), pp. 9–10.

3. John Mackinlay and Jarat Chopra, "Second Generation Multinational Operations," *The Washington Quarterly* 15, no. 3 (summer 1992): 113–131.

4. See for instance, Ruth B. Russell, *A History of The United Nations Charter: The Role of the United States 1940–1945* (Washington, D.C.: The Brookings Institution, 1958), especially chap. V.

5. Compare Thomas G. Weiss and Jarat Chopra, *United Nations Peacekeeping: An ACUNS Teaching Text* (Hanover, N.H.: Academic Council on the United Nations System, 1992); Alan James, *Peacekeeping in International Politics* (London: Macmillan and the International Institute for Strategic Studies, 1990); United Nations, *The Blue Helmets: A Review of United Nations Peacekeeping*, 2nd ed. (New York: United Nations Department of Public Information, 1990).

6. These were enunciated in the instructions for the establishment of the Second United Nations Emergency Force (UNEF II): "Report of the Secretary-General on the Implementation of Security Council Resolution 340 (1973)," UN Doc. S/11052/Rev. 1 of 27 October 1973. For a personal account of their drafting, see Brian Urquhart, *A Life in Peace and War* (New York: Harper and Row, 1987), pp. 241–242.

7. On the perceptions at the time of this critical mass point, see the special issue on "United Nations Peace-Keeping," Jarat Chopra, ed., *Survival* 32, no. 3 (May–June 1990).

8. See further John Mackinlay and Jarat Chopra, *A Draft Concept of Second Generation Multinational Operations, 1993* (Providence, R.I.: Thomas J. Watson Jr. Institute for International Studies, 1993).

9. Compare Jarat Chopra, "Achilles' Heel in Somalia: Learning from a Conceptual Failure," *Texas International Law Journal* 31, no. 3 (summer 1996): 495–525; Chopra, "Fighting for truth at the UN," *Crosslines Global Report* 4(8), no. 26 (November 1996): 7–9.

10. "Supplement to an Agenda for Peace: Position Paper of the Secretary-General on the Occasion of the Fiftieth Anniversary of the United Nations," UN Doc. A/50/60 and S/1995/1 of 3 January 1995, par. 36, par. 77–80.

11. UN Press Release SG/SM/5518 of 5 January 1995, pp. 5–6.

12. Compare Alan James, "Is there a second generation of peacekeeping?" *International Peacekeeping* 1, no. 4 (September–November 1994): 110–113; the panel on "UN Peacekeeping: An Early Reckoning of the Second Generation," *Proceedings of the American Society of International Law, 1995*, pp. 275–291; Boutros Boutros-Ghali, "Introduction," in United Nations, *The Blue Helmets*, 3d ed. (New York: United Nations Department of Public Information, 1996), p. 5; Commission of Inquiry into the Deployment of Canadian Forces to Somalia, *Dishonoured Legacy: The Lessons of the Somalia Affair*, Vol. 1 (Ottawa: Public Works and Government Services Canada, 1997), pp. 184–185.

13. Edmund T. Piasecki, "Making and Keeping the Peace," in John Tessitore and Susan Woolfson, eds., *A Global Agenda: Issues Before the 48th General Assembly of the United Nations* (Lanham, Md.: University Press of America, 1993), pp. 2, 3.

14. Compare Michael W. Doyle, *UN Peacekeeping in Cambodia: UNTAC's Civil Mandate* (Boulder: Lynne Rienner/International Peace Academy, 1995), pp. 76, 79.

15. Compare the casual usage in discussions at the General Assembly, UN Press Releases GA/SPD/77 of 15 November 1995, p. 4; GA/PK/137 of 1 April 1996, p. 8; and PI/993 WOM/953 of 7 March 1997, p. 2. Also compare the press usage in, for instance, Nirmal Mitra, "India Criticizes Unwelcome U.N. Help," *India Abroad*, 15 December 1995, p. 12, as opposed to Gilonne d'Origny, "Western Sahara's Difficult Path," *The Washington Times*, 3 July 1997, p. A17.

16. James A. Baker, III, *The Politics of Diplomacy: Revolution, War and Peace, 1989–1992* (New York: G.P. Putnam's Sons, 1995), p. xv.

17. On the articulation of the specific ingredients for this in a particular case, see Jarat Chopra, "A Chance for Peace in Western Sahara," *Survival* 39, no. 3 (autumn 1997): 51–65.

18. See further the debate on the feasibility and morality of peace-maintenance in Duane Bratt, "Rebuilding Fractured Societies," *Security Dialogue* 28, no. 2 (June 1997): 173–176, and Jarat Chopra, "The Peace-Maintenance Response," *Security Dialogue* 28, no. 2 (June 1997): 177–189.

19. Compare Ramsay Clark, *The Fire This Time: U.S. War Crimes In the Gulf* (New York: Thunder's Mouth Press, 1992); Kaiyan Homi Kaikobad, "Self-Defence, Enforcement Action and the Gulf Wars, 1980–88 and 1990–91," *British Year Book of International Law 1992*, (1993), pp. 333–335.

20. On the principles of this kind of activity, see further Chester Crocker, *High Noon In Southern Africa: Making Peace in a Rough Neighborhood* (New York: W.W. Norton & Company, 1992), chap. 19, 20.

21. Compare Jarat Chopra and Thomas G. Weiss, "Prospects for Containing Conflict in the Former Second World," *Security Studies* 4, no. 3 (spring 1995): 552–583.

2

Establishing Political Authority in Peace-Maintenance

⊕

W. Andy Knight

The demands on the UN system have increased noticeably since the end of the Cold War. Many of them, particularly those with a security dimension, happen to be qualitatively different from demands of the previous four decades. Yet the world organization continues to utilize old and worn doctrines in its response, even though the current global security situation cries out for new conceptualizations and approaches. This has led some to the conclusion that UN security mechanisms are in a state of crisis.[1]

John Gerard Ruggie, in a 1993 article in *Foreign Affairs*, described well the UN's post–Cold War security problematique: he said the organization had entered "a domain of military activity—a vaguely defined no-man's land lying somewhere between traditional peacekeeping and enforcement—for which it lacks any guiding operational concept. It has merely ratcheted up the traditional peacekeeping mechanism in an attempt to respond to wholly new security challenges."[2] As a result, UN peacekeepers continue to find themselves in contexts for which their limited function was never intended. Is there a way out of this dilemma for the UN, or are we witnessing what could be the end of the institution's role as a security organization?[3] Can we not develop more systematic approaches for dealing with international crises and conflicts?[4]

The Purpose of this Analysis

This chapter is not intended as a critical assessment of the overall peace-maintenance concept per se. Instead, it focuses on a central element of the concept; that is, the establishment of political authority by the international community as a means of linking strategic direction from the UN Security Council, General Assembly, and Secretariat with effective operations in the field, and as a conduit for the harmonization and coordination of diplomatic, military, humanitarian, and other civilian components of peace-maintenance operations. I propose the idea of an internationally

19

mandated political authority as an "ideal type," realizing that variations on the model can be conceptualized to suit the particular conflict arena.

It starts from the following assumptions: that the need for peace-maintenance has become urgent; that it is not sufficient to conceptualize peace-maintenance—there is also the need to develop a clear understanding of the nature of the political framework and context within which such a concept would be expected to operate; and that this requires an analysis of the dimensions of a peace-maintenance political authority, an understanding of the implications and requirements of establishing such an authority, and the measurement of the gap between the current state of peace operations and the capacity required for the establishment of the ideal peace-maintenance political authority, so that enlightened recommendation can be made as to how that chasm can be bridged.

This analysis therefore addresses the core of what is a peace-maintenance political authority, and what is entailed in establishing such an authority, by raising a number of questions. They are grouped under four analytical categories: dimensions, implications, requirements, and prospective evolution. It asks: What, precisely, are the tasks of a peace-maintenance authority? What means can be used to achieve those tasks? What groups, individuals, or other actors should, or can, be engaged in trying to achieve such tasks? What are the advantages of and difficulties associated with a peace-maintenance political authority? What are the ingredients necessary for its successful establishment? How far apart are the current state of peace operations and the capacity required for the establishment of an ideal peace-maintenance political authority? How can this gap be bridged?

Before answering these questions, it is important to put into perspective the prevailing need for a capability to establish peace-maintenance political authority. This is done by providing a thumbnail sketch of what can be perceived as a conceptual shift from the second generation model of multinational peace operations to the model of peace-maintenance.

The Conceptual Shift to Peace-Maintenance

Cambodia, Somalia, Bosnia, Rwanda, and Western Sahara all illustrate the limitations of the UN's current security approach and the need for a reconceptualization of global peace operations. While former Secretary-General Boutros Boutros-Ghali did make a valiant attempt, in *An Agenda for Peace*, to outline how the UN could respond to an obviously changing political and security context,[5] it has become evident that the world body, like other post–World War II institutions, has found itself caught between two paradigms—"the old order of stable strategic blocs and state sovereignty, and an emergent era of 'global governance.'"[6] During times of transition, the correct path to take is not always evident. Major powers, like the United States, have not been immune from this dilemma. They also find themselves groping for answers as they try to adapt their old strategic thinking and plans to a rapidly changing international environment. Thus, one ought to be sympathetic to the UN's "wandering in the void."

An expanded security concept,[7] coupled with the phenomenon of complex interdependence,[8] and the seemingly paradoxical trends of globalization and fragmentation, forced the UN security apparatus to adjust in ways for which it was not initially designed. Even the "add-on" security function of peacekeeping shifted its principles as troops, civilians, and nonstate actors deployed within states to address problems of intrastate conflicts—some say in direct contravention of Article 2(7), the nonintervention provision of the UN Charter. But what was the UN to do in the face of massive human rights abuses, genocidal acts, displacement of persons, mass starvation, and other humanitarian crises occurring within national boundaries? At times when the UN wanted to intervene to stop the internecine slaughter and fratricide, the traditional practice of obtaining consent from state parties and legitimate local authorities was not always possible, simply because state institutions had partially or completely collapsed.[9]

In several ruptured states, civil society needed protection from its national leaders and military establishment, or from the irregular forces attached to one power faction or another. As a way of circumventing Article 2(7), Chapter VII of the UN Charter—the explicit exception to nonintervention—was conveniently utilized to justify action. Consequently, several intrastate conflicts were designated, rightly or wrongly, "threats to international peace and security." The breakdown of law and order within states created man-made humanitarian emergencies and resulted in ethnic cleansing, guerrilla and irregular warfare, counterinsurgencies, and infrastructural damage, which tore apart the civil elements of a number of societies during this period. Internal conflicts proved much more complex than traditional interstate wars and required multifunctional responses—ranging from the use of military force to the distribution of humanitarian aid.

Under these new circumstances, it can be argued that the UN system did its best in representing the wishes of an international community sickened by the constant flashes on television of horrifying scenes from places like Angola, Haiti, Liberia, Rwanda, Somalia, and the former Yugoslavia. The so-called second generation of peace operations included multiple, but particularly military, means for bringing an end to violent and nascent conflict, ranging through the following: observation of cease-fire agreements; preventive deployment; demobilization and cantonment of warring factions and warlords; securing and/or confiscating their weapons; assisting interim civil authorities; helping resuscitate elements within civil society; supporting the monitoring and/or conduct of elections; facilitating the repatriation of refugees and relocation of displaced persons; mine clearing; protecting humanitarian relief operations; denying or guaranteeing rights of passage in international waterways and airspace, or across national territory; and arresting international criminals.[10] What was missing, however, was a comparable operational concept for coherent and comprehensive guidance, and an overall political framework that could better link the strategic and operational levels of command and control in the coordination of the various diplomatic, humanitarian, military, and civilian missions which the UN was undertaking.[11]

Jarat Chopra has developed a concept of peace-maintenance in an attempt to fill the doctrinal and practical void that has plagued UN second-generation peace operations.[12] One can become frustrated and wary of the ever expanding, and in some respects confusing, lexicon of "bluespeak," which includes: preventive diplomacy, peace-making, peacekeeping, preventive deployment, pre- and postconflict peace-building, and preventive peace-building. However, the notion of peace-maintenance does offer the possibility of crystallizing into a unified concept, with a coherent strategy and set of tactics for future UN peace operations. It purports to develop a mechanism for operational political direction and ongoing decisionmaking that functionally links UN headquarters with the field. As such, it may be indicative of a serious conceptual and doctrinal shift in the existing approach to the maintenance of international peace and security. Peace-maintenance, both proactively and reactively, provides short-, medium-, and long-term means of resolving violent and incipient disputes through the injection of an international political authority into local areas of conflict.

Peace-Maintenance and the
Establishment of Political Authority

Underlying the concept of peace-maintenance is a "hybrid" position that attempts to balance idealism and realism, and to subdue or minimize the extremes of euphoric hope and abject despair, which have alternated in the hearts and minds of scholars, practitioners, and lay people who have followed the fortunes of UN peace operations. The term peace-maintenance is used by Chopra in his introduction to mean specifically "the overall political framework, as part of which the objectives of diplomatic activities, humanitarian assistance, military forces, and civilian components are not only coordinated but harmonized." At the heart of this concept is the notion of establishing directly in the theater of conflict an internationally mandated political authority. This is considered the main ingredient missing in first- and second-generation peace missions. The goal of establishing a political authority is based on the assumption of a need to fulfill a political, executive function locally that would likely transform social conditions from violent or potential conflict and disorder to an environment in which the rule of law can be sustained.

Understanding "The Political" and "The Authority"

One of the frequently cited definitions of politics comes from David Easton, who asserted that it is a process through which societal values are authoritatively allocated.[13] However, this definition is too limited for our purposes, particularly if it is applied to the realm of the international. In this chapter, politics has to go beyond the authoritative allocation of values to include the restructuring of roles and relationships in society, the regulation of systems, the control of power bases, and the allocation of goods and services within a given polity. In other words, the "political" is what affects the operations of the state or its governance. It is concerned with issues of public affairs and civic administration. It has implications for the organized form of society. The "political" is therefore integrally linked to the "art of governing."

To govern is to rule with authority or to regulate, manage, and steer. The establishment of an internationally mandated political authority becomes necessary when the local people cannot agree on the ends their society should pursue, when there is a void of management and regulation, and when the local authority or leadership is either nonexistent or considered illegitimate. In such cases, the local people may need the presence of an external political authority to make decisions and to bring about a semblance of order until a new, legitimate, local government can be restored.

The word "authority" is also directly related to the notion of "governance," as used above in the description of "political." Authority relationships are generally defined in terms of "legitimacy" and "rightfulness." In this sense it must be considered both a philosophical and sociological concept. To ask questions about someone's authority is to ask a normative question about the right of that person to give a particular order, or to make a pronouncement, or to take a decision. The authority is therefore granted through a prior set of specific rules—constitutionally established or reached through conventions. We can treat the UN Charter as a body of rules that underwrite the authority of the international community. It reflects the minimal agreement within that community about the social values and principles that govern it, about the right way of doing things. It provides legitimacy for the actions of the organization and its members, as Sally Morphet points out in the next chapter.

Rwanda and the Need for "Outside" Political Authority

A distinction can be drawn between previous UN interventions and the idea of establishing a political authority in the local theater of conflict.

Chopra makes the argument that in the past, UN peace missions have been primarily of a diplomatic and/or military nature, but devoid of a true political dimension when deployed to their operational areas. To quote him directly, "the UN behaves as a diplomat and interlocutor, a representative of an authority far away, but fails to exercise political authority itself."[14] While one may disagree with the author's tendency to think of UN missions as being overly "diplomatic" and somehow not "political," one cannot help but agree with the empirical evidence that historically, in its operations, the UN has failed to establish effective political authority in the field.

A clear and appalling example is the case of Rwanda. The Arusha peace agreement was signed in August 1993 between the ruling Hutu government and the Tutsi-dominated Rwandan Patriotic Front (RPF). An impartial military force was to be deployed in the country within thirty-seven days to help implement the accords. A technical mission was sent by the UN to assess the operational needs. A reconnaissance mission, headed by the designated UN force commander, Gen. Romeo Dallaire of Canada, reported a mixed picture. On the one hand, it seemed that a classic Chapter VI and 1/2 UN peacekeeping force would be required. A peace agreement was signed, the local parties to the conflict had consented and cooperated, and both sides seemed willing to preserve the cease-fire, which was being monitored by regional and international observers—from the Organization of African Unity (OAU) and the UN Observer Mission Uganda-Rwanda (UNOMUR), respectively. Yet, on the other hand, General Dallaire was warning of potential major instability and dangers related to the fact that there was an unrealistically short period in which to deploy the operation. Given standard procedures, the UN needed between two to three months to assemble and deploy a peacekeeping force of the modest size proposed by the reconnaissance mission.

It took more than three months from the signing of the Arusha agreement for the first battalion to reach Rwanda. Militant forces in the country remained opposed to the accords and blocked the path of their implementation. In the meantime, disagreements between the UN Secretariat and Security Council about the size of the peacekeeping force led to further delays. The Secretariat estimated that 8,000 troops were needed. The United States, paying 31 percent of the total cost of the mission, insisted that a minimal force of 500 be sent to Rwanda. The French argued that 1,000 should suffice, given that their contingent in Kigali was only 600–700 men. General Dallaire's preferred force level was 4,500. In the end, it was agreed that 2,548 military personnel would be sent into the theater of conflict.[15]

Of course, in Rwanda the UN never established political authority, even though it could be argued that doing so in the country might have prevented the slaughter of close to a million people. Why was it unable to do this? The problem was partly due to immediately preceding events and partly to the UN's decisionmaking structures. With regard to the former, member governments seemed to have learned the wrong lessons from the Somalia debacle. One lesson should have been the organization's need to improve its rapid reaction capability and to develop an ability to establish quickly a political authority in the arena of conflict.[16] Instead, most UN member governments, particularly those on the Security Council, preferred to believe that the problem in Somalia had been "mission creep" and that in the future states would be reluctant to send their nations' troops to situations in which they had little or no strategic interest. For all but one of the major powers, Rwanda was only a peripheral concern. Regarding the latter part of the problem, structural shortcomings related to the cumbersome budgetary and deployment procedures at the UN, and the inability of the organization to adequately link political direction at headquarters with operational implementation.

The dramatic case of Rwanda should alert the international community to the need for ongoing decisionmaking in the field. The establishment of a peace-maintenance political authority is a means of preventing the escalation of violence and of creating an environment within which some semblance of normalcy can be achieved. But when and under what conditions should such an authority be established? What should be its specific tasks and what means can be used to achieve them? Who should establish this political authority and on what basis?

Dimensions Considered in
Establishing Political Authority

The need for establishing a peace-maintenance authority must be placed in the proper context. Introducing an outside political authority within the boundaries of a state can be justified only in the local absence of a legitimate political authority, and if the result has been societal chaos, violent conflict, indiscriminate killings, genocidal acts, massive human rights abuses, large outflows of refugees and displaced persons, or extraordinary institutional and infrastructural destruction. This is a rough description of a "failed state." According to I. William Zartman, when a state collapses, its structure, authority, law and order system, and political institutions simply fall apart.[17] Somalia, in the late 1980s and early 1990s, presented an example of the type of traumatic situation that could have benefited from an internationally mandated peace-maintenance mission.

Somalia and the "Failed State" Syndrome

By the end of the 1980s, with shrinking political support, Mohammed Siyad Barre, the dictator of Somalia since 1969, depended increasingly on repressive measures to counter threats to his personal power base. But, ultimately, he did not succeed. After his intensive bombing campaign against the northern towns in 1988, the opposition Somali National Movement (SNM) managed to regroup and continue its nearly decade-long armed resistance. It cut the vital roads to the north and recruited from Issaq clans in the northeast for its insurgency. The SNM's success was matched by the Somali Patriotic Movement (SPM), which gradually took over the country's southern region. There were also some newcomers to the competition. One of them was the United Somali Congress (USC), organized by the Hawiye—the predominant clan in the center of the country and especially the capital, Mogadishu. The USC was founded in January 1989 by Ali Mohamed Wardingly, formerly elected vice-chair of the SNM in 1984 but removed three years later.[18] Wardingly's response to being sacked by the SNM was to create the USC. However, members of the Habar Gidir, a subclan of the Hawiye, chose to remain associated with the SNM. This faction, led by Gen. Mohammed Farah Aideed, would eventually take over parts of the USC and then separate as the Somali National Alliance (SNA). Aideed came to occupy a preeminent position in Somalia's conflict, primarily because of his Hawiye stronghold in Mogadishu—where the civil war was fought most fiercely.

Intensification of the conflict in many parts of the country paralyzed economic activity. Livestock exports from the northern region, which in the past accounted for nearly 80 percent of total foreign export, came to a virtual halt as a result of the SNM's control of the rural areas and the negative consequences of the 1988 fighting. By the end of 1989, the state-run banking system was near collapse. In November that year, five junior banking officials were sentenced to death, having been found guilty of embezzling 75 million Somali shillings.[19] In the meantime, Somalia's external debt rose far above manageable levels. It was estimated that debt service 1988–1990 amounted to $120 million per year. In the meantime, the exchange rate fell quickly. A typical civil servant's monthly salary, worth $60 two years previous, could not buy even two cans of beer.[20] Added to this, the United States suspended virtually all aid to Somalia.

The defection of government soldiers to the different opposition movements became a common occurrence, as antigovernment agitation continued to spread throughout Mogadishu. In December 1990 and January 1991, USC and SPM forces closed in on the capital. The beleaguered president began a strategy of instigating fighting inside the city between members of his Darod clan—many of whom he had armed—and the Hawiye supporters of the USC. Meanwhile, negotiations began with the so-called Manifesto Group, and some of their members were appointed to a new government created by Barre. Other members of the Manifesto Group, who were left out of this arrangement, organized armed resistance inside Mogadishu in the form of a new wing of the USC. The rebels wore white head bands so they could recognize one another, but no one else knew whether they were government soldiers (known as Faqash), rebel guerrillas, or civilians. Negotiations and appeals for cease-fires from the European Community, Italy, and Egypt failed to produce any calm.[21]

On 19 January 1991, USC forces under the command of General Aideed entered Mogadishu. The capital was ravaged by fighting between government troops and rebel forces. Tanks were burned, main streets blocked, and shops and banks looted. Foreigners began to escape the violence. On 26 January, after roughly one month of bloody combat, USC forces drove Siyad Barre out of Mogadishu. Three days later, prominent members of the Manifesto Group formed a government, with Ali Mahdi Mohammed, a local businessman, appointed as interim president. The decision was defended by the group on the grounds that they had been fighting in the city to depose Barre for three weeks before General Aideed arrived, "very late in the day" to claim the fruits of the victory that was rightfully theirs.[22] This unwise decision to mount Ali Mahdi as the new provisional head of the Somali government would serve only to exacerbate tensions in the country, and to precipitate an even more serious round in the civil war and an eventual disintegration of authority.

This brief account of state collapse in Somalia indicates the conditions under which an internationally mandated political authority might be established. Viewed from the "failed state" perspective, the broad tasks of peace-maintenance might be categorized temporally, in *immediate, medium,* and *long* terms.

Immediate tasks of the political authority. The immediate task of a peace-maintenance political authority should be to dispatch to the theater of conflict a rapid reaction military and diplomatic unit, including an operational-level headquarters comprised of military and civilian personnel. With the aim of deescalating the conflict and containing the crisis, it would utilize its diplomatic personnel to broker a cease-fire agreement between the warring parties, and monitor that cease-fire with the assistance of military forces. These could be configured as a preventive deployment or—if the local atmosphere is relatively calm—as a more conventional peacekeeping force, or even an observer unit. Additionally, troops may need to: provide security for humanitarian convoys of UN agencies and nongovernmental organizations, and for those displaced persons wishing to return to their homes; disarm warring factions and demobilize irregular troops; and clear land mines.

The civilian authority needs to: set up an independent means of law enforcement and an independent prosecutorial office to investigate international criminal activity; dispatch human rights officers throughout the country to monitor and report on human rights violations; operate an office of legal experts to assist in constitutional interpretation, among other things; and, above all, establish a joint decisionmaking body comprised of individuals from the internationally mandated political authority and those from local rival groups. At this stage, the purpose of these tasks is preventive—to lower the level and intensity of the conflict and guarantee sufficiently the cessation of hostilities, so that negotiations can take place between the emerging local authorities and the peace-maintenance authority.

Medium-term tasks of the political authority.   Among the medium-term tasks of the political authority should be: the administration of necessary and basic state services, ministries, and agencies; the revivification of civil society and its institutions; the repatriation of refugees and displaced persons; the introduction of confidence-building measures that stimulate rapprochement and encourage dialogue between belligerents; the initiation of transitional processes, such as the organization and preparation of elections; the consolidation of internal and external security by training and restructuring a local police force and a skeletal armed force; the drawing up of an electoral list and the training of returning officers; the administration and monitoring of the electoral process, ensuring that all factions that want to participate are represented; the rehabilitation of basic infrastructure (such as roads, bridges, health and education services, water and sanitation systems, irrigation systems, commercial outlets, and telecommunication systems); the coordination of external aid, economic packages, and technical assistance, as a means of promoting economic and social revitalization; the implementation of environmental protection plans (such as soil conservation, reforestation, flood control, wildlife management, and pollution controls); the establishment of civilian control over the local military and police forces; and the establishment of national and provincial courts as part of an independent judiciary.

The main purpose of peace-maintenance tasks at this stage, once there is a period of sustained calm, is to facilitate a smooth transition from the international to the local control of political authority. After all, the purpose of the international political authority is not to become a neocolonial power, as emphasized in the early pages of and throughout this book. A subsidiary goal of the medium-term tasks may be comparable to "peace-building." This should result not only in the reestablishment of the state apparatus but, more importantly, in the revivification of the civil society. It takes a thriving civil society to produce a legitimate and democratic government.

Long-term tasks of the political authority.   The long-term tasks of the international political authority should be geared toward facilitating national reconciliation, establishing "truth commissions," empowering civil society, and engaging in postconflict institutional training and reform. It is by this point that most elements of governance should have been transferred to a legitimate local authority. The emphasis at this stage should be a longer-term strategy for ensuring the political and economic stability needed for the avoidance of a descent back into violence.[23] Tasks should be designed to consolidate the peace, and might include the development and implementation of a program of human rights education and the oversight of human rights law implementation. Critical to the success of long-term goals is the investigation and understanding of the root causes of the conflict.

These lists of tasks are meant to be indicative and not exhaustive. And, certainly, the specifics of peace-maintenance will vary depending on the degree of collapse in the target state. The next set of questions to be resolved relate to the means and actors that can be utilized to achieve such tasks and the basis upon which a political authority can be established.

Means, Actors, and the Legitimating Source

A direct link exists between authority structures and the issue of legitimacy. The authority of a political body may not be recognized if that authority does not have a source of legitimacy. Rational-legal authority is bestowed through impersonal rules, the existence of which can be justified on more or less rational grounds. Alternatively, traditional authority may be based on unwritten, but internally binding, rules arrived at through historical precedent rather than necessarily by a rational process. The authority of the tribal chief is one example of this. Another form of authority is charismatic authority, which appears to be unrelated to rules but can be explained in terms of personal qualities of an individual that entitle him or her to obedience.[24] All three of these Weberian ideal types of authority may be exhibited in peace-maintenance. But what would give this international authority its legitimacy?

The establishment of legitimate political authority in a peace-maintenance venture requires a mandate from the international community, in the form of a resolution of either the UN Security Council or the General Assembly. Chopra asserts that if "peace-maintenance is to be successfully developed, then it must be collectively underwritten by the international community as a whole."[25] This is the source of its legitimacy. The legal framework for peace-maintenance, as Chopra also points out, can be found in Article 1(1) of the UN Charter. According to this, the international body may use effective collective measures for the prevention and removal of threats to the peace, the suppression of acts of aggression or breaches of the peace, and the adjustment or settlement of actual or incipient international disputes. The recommended means is through the utilization of peaceful measures, used in conformity with principles of justice and international law.

Article 1(2) adds that the UN should help develop friendly relations among nations based on respect for the principle of equal rights and the self-determination of peoples, and that it should strengthen universal peace through the use of "appropriate measures." Article 1(4) states that the UN should become the center for harmonizing the actions of nations to achieve the above ends. How precisely this is to be done is left open to the UN membership.

The UN system could try to accomplish most of this on its own. However, it is in perpetual financial crisis and overburdened after the Cold War, particularly with regards to the expanded scope of its peace and security functions. Therefore, one might draw on the provisions of Chapter VIII of the UN Charter to identify the kinds of actors that could participate in the operations of a peace-maintenance political authority.[26]

Utilizing the subsidiarity principle. Although the UN Charter gives primary responsibility to the Security Council for the maintenance of international peace and security, Chapter VIII allots at least the sharing of that role with "regional arrangements or agencies." There is some ambiguity about whether this refers to informal, ad hoc mechanisms or constituted organizations. Nevertheless, the founding fathers had a particular vision of what should be the division of labor between the UN system and regional bodies. In the event a local dispute erupted, UN member nations in the proximate geographical location would be expected under Article 52(2), if they were part of a regional arrangement or agency, to "make every effort to achieve pacific settlement of local disputes through such regional arrangements or by such regional agencies before referring them to the Security Council."

This secondary role is encouraged by the council, as long as it does not impair the UN's ability under Article 34 to investigate independently and decide whether or not the local dispute might escalate and threaten international peace and security, or pose any obstacle to a member of the UN that wishes to bring a dispute to the attention of the council under Article 35. According to Article 53(1) of Chapter VIII, the Security Council can utilize regional agents to carry out "enforcement action under its authority." However, no such enforcement can be undertaken by regional arrangements or agencies "without the authorization" of the council. As if to emphasize that all regional action ought to be under the umbrella of the UN, Article 54 requires that the council be kept informed of security activities undertaken or contemplated by regional bodies.

Chapter VIII is already operational to some degree. As James Sutterlin points out, formal agreements already exist between the UN and several regional bodies, such as the OAU, the League of Arab States (LAS), and the Organization of the Islamic Conference (OIC). Other regional bodies have declared themselves Chapter VIII regional arrangements or agencies. For instance, the Conference (now Organization) on Security and Cooperation in Europe (OSCE) made such an announcement in 1992. Other regional organizations have observer status at the UN, including the European Union.[27] Also, there have been cases in which the UN has authorized a regional organization to carry out a peace-enforcement action, as illustrated by the North Atlantic Treaty Organization (NATO) bombing in Bosnia to protect "safe havens."[28]

Although the UN has played the dominant role in many regional conflicts (in Iran-Iraq, Afghanistan, Nicaragua, Angola, Cambodia, Somalia, Haiti, Mozambique, Rwanda, Western Sahara, and the former Yugoslavia), on occasion it has taken a back seat to a regional body, like the Economic Community of West African States (ECOWAS) and its Monitoring Group (ECOMOG) in Liberia.[29] Elsewhere, the UN has shared its conflict resolution role with key individuals and regional organizations, as in the implementation of the Esquipulas agreements. Stephen Baranyi and Liisa North explain that in August 1989 in Tela, Honduras, marking the second anniversary of Esquipulas II, five Central American presidents requested that the secretaries-general of both the UN and the Organization of American States (OAS) establish an International Support and Verification Commission (CIAV) "to assist in the demobilization of the contras." In principle, the labor was divided in the following manner: the UN Observer Group in Central America (ONUCA) was authorized to "monitor on a regular basis areas reported to harbour bases and camps of irregular forces"; while CIAV was mandated by the OAS "to receive the arms, equipment, and military supplies of the Nicaraguan Resistance and of other irregular forces that might wish to demobilize voluntarily."[30]

Sutterlin adds that the OAS has even had some success in resolving regional disputes without the help of the UN, between: Costa Rica and Nicaragua (1948–1949, 1955–1956, and 1959); Honduras and Nicaragua (1957); Venezuela and the Dominican Republic (1960–1961); Venezuela and Cuba (1963–1964 and 1967); the Dominican Republic and Haiti (1950 and 1963–1965); Panama and the United States (1964); and El Salvador and Honduras (1960–1970).[31] The Association of Southeast Asian Nations (ASEAN) had limited results with the UN's help in bringing together the various parties in the Cambodian conflict to seek a way of ending their violence in the early 1990s.

On the other hand, the OAU has not had much success in preventive diplomacy or peace-making efforts on the African continent. The only African country that has modern armed forces is South Africa. However, President Nelson Mandela has been reluctant to have his country coercively intervene in other African states. The attempts of the OAU to resolve the problems in Chad and Western Sahara served to show the extent of its lack of resources and internal cohesion, and its inability to develop consensus amongst its member states about the conditions for both the establishment and deployment of forces. In 1993, on the thirtieth anniversary of the founding of the OAU, the fifty-two heads of state and government of the organization renewed their determination "to work in concert in search for speedy and peaceful resolution to all the conflicts in Africa."[32] But they recognized that the primary emphasis would have to be given to anticipatory and preventive action to obviate the need to become involved in complex and drawn-out peacekeeping operations, which tend to be difficult for these countries to finance. Subsequently, its inaction in the Rwandan crisis led to a French intervention in 1994 and to the charge that "Africans are unwilling to help themselves."[33]

Perhaps embarrassed by this situation, the OAU met in Biarritz, France, in November 1994, to discuss the formation of a regional peacekeeping force that would be made available for operations throughout the African continent. Plans were drawn up for the creation of a standing force of between one thousand and fifteen hundred soldiers from each OAU contributing country, to be equipped and financed by France, other European powers, and possibly the United States. The aim behind this proposal is for the OAU to develop the competence to deal with its security problems so that the UN, which has already deployed thirty-two thousand troops in Africa, would not have to intervene every time violence breaks out. More importantly, members of the OAU are openly worried about the precedent that France's intervention in Rwanda may set for the future. This has resulted in a concerted effort on the part of its members to develop a conflict prevention mechanism for Africa, including the establishment of a conflict management center at the OAU.[34] Also, the Clinton administration is sending teams of army Green Beret soldiers to train eight battalion-size military units from seven African nations in peace operations and humanitarian relief. The U.S. program complements similar efforts by Britain and France.[35]

This analysis shows that although there are weaknesses in the security capability of many regional bodies, they do not prevent some form of collaboration or joint action between the UN and regional arrangements and agencies in peace-maintenance efforts. Such subsidiarity arrangements might be required for good reason. As a cautionary note, however, it would be important to guard against self-interested actions by regional lead-nations or coalitions exercising international political powers. If a conflict erupts in a particular region, as in Africa, the local people most directly affected will probably have the final say in how it ends. They are the ones who suffer the immediate consequences of the fighting, the refugee flows, the social dislocation, and the economic losses. They have the greatest stake in the management, resolution, and outcome of the conflict. Those close to the fighting, if they are not direct combatants, also may be in a better position to mediate between warring parties. In most cases, they are less ethnocentric than intervenors from other regions. They may have personal connections to the protagonists in the conflict, and as Neil MacFarlane and Thomas Weiss put it, "issues relating to local conflict are far more likely to be given full and urgent consideration in regional fora than in global ones, since the latter have broader agendas, competing priorities, and numerous distractions."[36]

Thus, it is possible that the actors involved in the operations of an internationally mandated political authority could range from the UN system independently, to joint action between the UN and a regional arrangement or agency, to a delegated regional body on its own—as long as it acts with the consent of the international community. There is no reason why a group of states could not be similarly delegated the tasks of a UN-authorized political authority.

Implications: Advantages and Drawbacks of a Peace-Maintenance Political Authority

It is easy to identify the advantages of an "ideal type" of peace-maintenance political authority. Integration and harmonization of international diplomatic, military, and humanitarian activities, as part of an overall political strategy, would provide the much sought-after unity of purpose in the field. Ongoing decisionmaking on the ground, as a result of unity of civilian command and control, would make possible a rapidly deployable, effective and coordinated presence in "failed states." Being physically present, statically, in such a theater of conflict is not enough; a political authority is able to address dynamically the problems that gave rise to the conflict in the first place. It can introduce multifunctional means of tackling complex emergencies, by using: preventive measures; observation; peacekeeping; military force; humanitarian assistance; confidence-building measures; and techniques of conflict resolution, and peace and state building.

After restoring some semblance of order, an international political authority in a war-torn society is able to begin the process of resuscitating the institutions of civil society, relocating the displaced, revitalizing the economy, rebuilding damaged infrastructure, and establishing the foundations upon which government institutions can be revived or newly created. This comprehensive, holistic approach to controlling violent conflict is a marked advantage over the piecemeal, segregated approaches of first- and second-generation peace operations. However, peace-maintenance does have its drawbacks.

First, if, as some scholars argue, most of the post–Cold War conflicts are sui generis, then the establishment of an "outside" political authority in a theater of conflict will certainly not be unproblematic. Would the local populations in any of the current failed states readily accept the presence in their country of an external authority? In his chapter, Clement Adibe warns that there is a good possibility such intervention will be viewed, particularly in the Third World, as a form of neocolonialism or neoimperialism.

Reliance on the Security Council as the sole legitimator of peace-maintenance may exacerbate this image.

Second, civil wars are generally very complicated affairs with unique features and, in some instances, multiple root causes. Chester A. Crocker argues that "it is common knowledge that it is especially difficult for outsiders to manage internal conflicts. Familiarity of the sort acquired in civil wars appears to breed a special contempt for the enemy and a heightened incentive for aggressive brutality. . . . The superficial implication is that outsiders would be well-advised to steer clear of trying to manage such affairs."[37]

Third, while it may seem justifiable for the international community to inject into a clearly "failed state" a peace-maintenance political authority, it may be more difficult to justify such an intervention if the war-torn society still had some semblance of its legitimate government intact. Despite the existence of empirical knowledge that juridical sovereignty is not what it used to be, many states are still loath to engage in any operation that crosses the sovereignty line of another.

Finally, would such a political authority be allowed on the territory of a major state or middle power if there was an outbreak of violence and disorder? The answer to this question is most likely "no." One cannot but empathize with those peoples from marginalized states who fear that such inventions as rapid reaction forces or governorship-in-trust arrangements are designed to target the poor, the underdeveloped, and the underprivileged within the international system. In other words, there is a perception that such concepts will be applied in a hypocritical and one-sided manner.

Requirements and Ingredients
for Establishing Political Authority

As mentioned earlier, the first and most important ingredient required for the establishment of a peace-maintenance political authority is a mandate from the international community. Without such approval from either the UN Security Council or General Assembly, or both, it would be difficult for the local population in the war-torn area to accept this "outside" authority. Building local authority is an intensely political act that requires adequate attention to sources of legitimation, forms of political empowerment, and problems associated with ethnic and national reconciliation. Its success or failure also may hinge on the degree to which a subsidiarity arrangement is employed.

The second requirement would be the harnessing of political will, as well as financial and human resources, for carrying out the tasks of the political authority. This may mean that some states will have to decide whether or not to commit to the management and resolution of conflicts in which they have no interest. It will be necessary in such cases for the state leaders to somehow view far-away conflicts as having at least an indirect impact on their own peoples. It may also require that state leaders think not so much in national policy terms but rather in global polity terms. This in turn requires consciousness-raising.

The third requirement is the development of a rapid reaction capability for the international community. It is difficult for a political authority to be effectively inserted into a theater of conflict without this. The generic components of a rapid reaction competence include: an early warning mechanism; an effective decisionmaking process; a readily available transportation unit and infrastructure; adequate logistical support; adequate finances; and well-trained personnel. These are not yet present within the UN system.

Linked to the above, an eventual fourth requirement should be a permanent UN police and military force. Reliance on the current ad hoc arrangement for putting together national contingents and subcontracting to potentially self-interested coalitions will not do. As Rwanda indicated, a standing UN force could save thousands of lives if it were deployed rapidly. A permanent force would have to operate under UN command. This realization has led some scholars to suggest that such a global force would have to be recruited directly from among volunteers of individual countries. Members of the force also would be required to undergo cultural, regional, and religious sensitivity training.[38]

Finally, the personnel of a peace-maintenance political authority would have to be drawn from all walks of life. The multifunctional nature of the authority's operations require that the pool of employees could come from, among others, legal, business, educational, engineering, computer, telecommunications, governmental, nongovernmental, environmental, medical, scientific and religious backgrounds.

Conclusion

Failure to reconceptualize and redesign the UN's role in the area of maintaining international peace and security could result in the end of the world body as a security organization. Jarat Chopra and the other authors in this volume have begun a process of reconceptualization and redesign with the aim of moving toward legitimate and effective peace-maintenance. This is a concept that recognizes the need for the exercise of political authority by the international community in the quest for global governance—and the harmonization of its diplomatic, military, humanitarian, and civilian aspects. As such, peace-maintenance is explicitly designed to transcend the parochial interests of nation-state politics and is aimed at developing forms of political action based on the notion of cosmopolitan interests.

Will the UN system be in a position in the near future to bring about the realization of this concept? What gaps need to be bridged between the current state of peace operations and the capacity required for the establishment of a peace-maintenance political authority?

In countries where the UN has intervened because of the collapse of a government, the organization has been reluctant to assume the responsibilities of governing. For the most part, the UN's role has been limited to offering administrative assistance, training, organizing and monitoring elections, and giving advice. But in cases where a government does not exist, the results of such efforts tend not to survive. The issue of more direct and comprehensive administration and overall governance in such states by the international body is one that has to be addressed. This raises the prospects of trusteeship-like arrangements.[39] There may be major objections from those who could possibly be subjected to this form of international political authority and perceive it as neocolonialism or neoimperialism. Most of these people are represented at the UN and, collectively, they form a formidable bloc in the General Assembly, which can derail attempts to implement such notions.

Those who have been following the fortunes of the UN over the years know some of the problems that will need to be overcome if the world organization is to become a central player in any rearticulated international security arrangement. The UN still lacks the command and control capabilities to manage peace operations effectively. It is hindered by an arcane organizational structure and a set of cumbersome operating procedures. The UN must depend on its member states to supply military troops and civilian personnel for its missions. The multinational nature of these operations makes them difficult to manage, because of the different working languages, equipment, procedures, and levels of military training. Some countries, like the United States, have made it quite clear that their forces will not be placed under UN command for the foreseeable future. Some unit commanders within UN operations generally seek approval from home governments before committing their countries' troops to particular actions in the field, especially when the use of coercive force is involved. Those field commanders who operate in the spirit or the letter of the UN Charter complain at times that they have too little authority to take action without the explicit permission of UN headquarters. It is also well known that officials in New York generally lack the necessary understanding of conditions in the field to make informed decisions and judgments. Finally, the Byzantine procurement system of the UN prevents the organization from quickly obtaining the equipment and supplies that it needs for its field operations, while the deliberate withholding by the United States of its assessed contributions to the UN regular and peacekeeping budgets threatens to push the organization into a state of insolvency.

The situation is not, however, entirely bleak. Already a few institutional reforms have been adopted in response to the above problems, including:

1. The creation within the Department of Peace-Keeping Operations (DPKO) of a mission planning service to coordinate the predeployment planning of operations and training of peacekeepers. This division has published standardized peacekeeping training modules and developed "training assistance teams" for countries requesting advice on the training of personnel for UN operations.
2. The Field Administration and Logistics Division was incorporated into DPKO to improve the consistency of headquarters' communications with the field.
3. The UN continues to expand its "standby arrangements." There are now fifty-four member states that have concluded such agreements with the UN, thus earmarking troops and resources for possible use in peace operations.
4. The organization is developing a "rapidly deployable headquarters team" within the Secretariat—one of the proposals from the Canadian *Rapid Reaction* study—which would conduct advance planning for operations and then form the nucleus of a new mission's field headquarters, thus improving continuity between planning and implementation phases of UN operations.
5. A twenty-four–hour situation center was established in New York and it maintains constant contact with field operations.
6. A "lessons-learned" unit has been created supposedly to distill the lessons of previous operations and recommend further institutional reforms based on those experiences.
7. The UN has established a logistics depot at Brindisi, Italy, to store UN materiel and provide "start-up kits" of equipment for quick deployment to new missions, and a medical supplies depot in Oslo.
8. The organization has introduced a more flexible budgeting process for UN field operations.[40]

In July 1997, Secretary-General Kofi Annan unveiled a comprehensive reform package for the organization. Some of the proposals that could have implications for more effective peace-maintenance include: the creation of a strategic planning unit; the promise of a "development dividend"—a reallocation of savings from administrative cuts to developmental activities; the establishment of a revolving credit fund; the allocation of funds and programs directly to a UN development group, as a means of enhancing the Secretariat's ability to promote sustainable development and thus tackle root causes of poverty and conflict; the creation of the Office for Development Financing; and the designation of the Department of Political Affairs (DPA) as the focal point for strengthening the postconflict peace-building capacity of the organization.[41]

These changes indicate that the UN is in the process of modifying its approach to security from one that was almost entirely reactive, during the Cold War and the immediate post–Cold War era, to one that proactively sets out to secure, in areas of conflict, conditions of peace that can be supported and sustained in the long term. Despite this, it would seem that the UN is still a long way from the establishment of an international political authority. ⊕

Notes

W. Andy Knight is assistant professor of political studies at Bishop's University in Lennoxville, Québec. Currently serving as vice-chair of the Academic Council on the United Nations System, he is editor (with Keith Krause) of *State, Society and the UN System* (Tokyo: United Nations University, 1995).

1. See Adam Roberts, "The Crisis in UN Peacekeeping," in Chester A. Crocker and Fen Osler Hampson, with Pamela Aall, eds., *Managing Global Chaos: Sources of and Responses to International Conflict* (Washington, D.C.: United States Institute of Peace Press, 1996), pp. 297–319.

2. John Gerard Ruggie, "Wandering in the Void: Charting the U.N.'s New Strategic Role," *Foreign Affairs* 72, no. 5 (November-December 1993): 26.

3. See Roland Paris, "Blue Helmet Blues: The End of the UN as a Security Organization?" *The Washington Quarterly* 20, no.1 (1996): 191–206.

4. Other scholars and practitioners are thinking along similar lines of developing more systematic approaches for the prevention of deadly conflict, although with different emphases. See for example, Andrew J. Goodpastor, *When Diplomacy is not Enough: Managing Multinational Military Interventions*, A Report of the Carnegie Commission on Preventing Deadly Conflict (New York: Carnegie Corporation of New York, July 1996); Michael S. Lund, *Preventing Violent Conflicts: A Strategy for Preventive Diplomacy* (Washington, D.C.: United States Institute of Peace Press, 1996); and Crocker et al., *Managing Global Chaos*.

5. Boutros Boutros-Ghali, *An Agenda for Peace: Preventive Diplomacy, Peacemaking and Peace-Keeping* (New York: United Nations Department of Public Information, 1992).

6. See David R. Black, "Towards Multilateral Conflict Prevention and Resolution," in David R. Black and Susan J. Rolston, eds., *Peacemaking and Preventive Diplomacy in the New World (Dis) Order* (Halifax, N.S.: Centre for Foreign Policy Studies, Dalhousie University, July 1995), p. 3.

7. For a recent review of the literature on this point, see Keith Krause and Michael Williams, "Broadening the Agenda of Security Studies: Politics and Methods," *Mershon International Studies Review* 40, supplement 2 (October 1996): 229–254.

8. See Robert Keohane and Joseph Nye, *Power and Interdependence: World Politics in Transition* (Boston, Mass.: Little Brown, 1977).

9. For an excellent study of this phenomenon of failed states, see I. William Zartman, ed., *Collapsed States: The Disintegration and Restoration of Legitimate Authority* (Boulder: Lynne Rienner, 1995).

10. For a good overview of several examples of these, see John Tessitore and Susan Woolfson, eds., *A Global Agenda: Issues Before the 51st General Assembly of the United Nations* (New York: University Press of America, 1996); Jarat Chopra, Åge Eknes, and Toralv Nordbø, *Fighting for Hope in Somalia* (Oslo: Norwegian Institute of International Affairs, 1995); James S. Sutterlin, *The United Nations and the Maintenance of International Security: A Challenge to be Met* (London: Praeger, 1995); Janet E. Heininger, *Peacekeeping in Transition: The United Nations in Cambodia* (New York: Twentieth Century Fund Press, 1994).

11. Jarat Chopra, "Back to the Drawing Board," *The Bulletin of the Atomic Scientists* 51, no. 2 (March-April 1995): 29–35.

12. Jarat Chopra, "The Space of Peace-Maintenance," *Political Geography* 15, no. 3/4 (March-April 1996): 335–357; and on the second generation of UN peace operations, see John Mackinlay and Jarat Chopra, "Second Generation Multinational Operations," *The Washington Quarterly* 15, no. 3 (summer 1992): 113–131.

13. David Easton, *The Political System* (New York: Knopf, 1959), pp. 129–131.

14. Chopra, "The Space of Peace-Maintenance," p. 338.

15. For a more in-depth examination of this case, see Howard Adelman and Astri Suhrke, with Bruce Jones, *Early Warning and Conflict Management: Genocide in Rwanda*, Study II of the Evaluation of Emergency Assistance to Rwanda (Fantoft-Bergen, Norway: CHR Michelsen Institute—Development Studies and Human Rights, September 1995).

16. See the Report of the Government of Canada, *Towards a Rapid Reaction Capability for the United Nations* (Ottawa: The Government of Canada, September 1995).

17. Zartman, *Collapsed States*, p. 1.

18. "Somalia: Where Do We Go From Here?" *Africa Confidential*, 32, no. 3 (8 February 1991): 1.

19. Margaret Dolley, "Somalia: Economy," *Africa: South of the Sahara 1991*, 20th ed. (England: Europa Publications, 1991), p. 904.

20. "Somalia: the Mayor of Mogadishu," *The Economist*, 29 September 1990, p. 47.

21. Foreign Broadcast Information Service, "Italian, Egyptian Diplomats On Reconciliation", *FBIS*, 6 May 1991, p. 10.

22. Africa Watch interview with Awyes Haji Yusuf in the presidential office of the interim government, 2 February 1992, cited in Africa Watch, *Somalia: A Fight to the Death?* 4, no. 2 (13 February 1992): 4.

23. On the stages of political order and state collapse, see further Jarat Chopra, "Peace-Maintenance: The Last Stage of Development," *Global Society* 11, no. 2 (May 1997): 185–204.

24. Norman P. Barry, *An Introduction to Modern Political Theory*, 2d ed. (London: Macmillan, 1989), pp. 81–89.

25. Chopra, "The Space of Peace-Maintenance," p. 355.

26. See W. Andy Knight, "Towards a Subsidiarity Model for Peacemaking and Preventive Diplomacy: Making Chapter VIII of the UN Charter Operational," *Third World Quarterly* 17, no.1 (March 1996): 31–52.

27. See Sutterlin, *The United Nations and the Maintenance of International Security*, pp. 93–112.

28. UN Security Council Resolution 836 of 4 June 1993.

29. For good reviews of this case, see Clement E. Adibe, "The Liberian Conflict and the ECOWAS-UN Partnership," *Third World Quarterly* 18, no. 3 (1997): 471–488; and James O. Jonah, "ECOMOG: A Successful Example of Peacemaking

and Peacekeeping by a Regional Organization in the Third World," in W. Kühne, ed., *Internationales Umfeld, Sicherheitsinteressen und Nationale Planung der Bundesrepublik* (Ebenhausen: Stiftung Wissenschaft und Politik, 1993), pp. 197–217.

30. Stephen Baranyi and Liisa North, *Stretching the Limits of the Possible: United Nations Peacekeeping in Central America*, Aurora Papers, No. 15 (Ottawa: Canadian Centre for Global Security, 1992).

31. Sutterlin, *The United Nations and the Maintenance of International Security*, pp. 95–97.

32. OAU, "Declaration of the Assembly of the Heads of State and Government on the Establishment within the OAU of a Mechanism for Conflict Prevention, Management and Resolution," AHG/Decl.3 (xxix), rev. 1 (29th Ordinary Session in Cairo, Egypt, June 28–30, 1993), especially pp. 4–6.

33. See "National Notations," *Peacekeeping & International Relations* 24, no.1 (January-February 1995): 13.

34. See further, William Godwin Nhara, "Early Warning and Conflict in Africa," *Institute for Defence Policy Papers*, no. 1, February 1996, pp. 2–3, and generally.

35. Thomas W. Lippman, "U.S. Ready to Train African Peacekeepers," *The Washington Post*, 30 June 1997, p. A16. Note that the seven African states involved are: Uganda, Senegal, Tunisia, Ethiopia, Mali, Malawi and Ghana.

36. S. Neil MacFarlane and Thomas G. Weiss, "The United Nations, Regional Organizations, and Human Security: Building Theory in Central America" in Luís Guillermo Solís et al., eds., *Regional Responsibilities and the United Nations System* (Providence, R.I.: Academic Council on the United Nations System, 1994), p. 25.

37. Chester A. Crocker, "The Varieties of Intervention: Conditions for Success," in Crocker et al., *Managing Global Chaos*, p. 184.

38. Robert Johansen, "The Future of United Nations Peacekeeping and Enforcement: A Framework for Policymaking," *Global Governance* 2, no. 3 (September-December 1996): 317.

39. See, for instance, Peter Lyon, "The Rise and Fall and Possible Revival of International Trusteeship," *Journal of Commonwealth and Comparative Politics* 31 (March 1993): 96–110.

40. See Paris, "Blue Helmet Blues," pp. 200–201.

41. See further Kofi Annan's Track Two proposals in the Secretary-General's report to the General Assembly on "Renewing the United Nations: Programme for Reform," UN Doc. A/51/1950 of 16 July 1997. Also, see Barbara Crossette, "U.N. Chief Promises to Overhaul Organization From the Top Down," *The New York Times*, 17 July 1997, pp. A1, A12.

3

Organizing Civil Administration in Peace-Maintenance

———————— ⊕ ————————

Sally Morphet

The aim of this chapter is to survey the way the UN has assumed a range of civil administration tasks in the context of certain peace-keeping and peace-enforcement operations. It discusses how this has worked in practice and considers the technical and political lessons that can be learned from each mission. The chapter also evaluates what has helped these operations achieve political legitimacy at an international and national level—a critical element of peace-maintenance—and tries to identify future trends.

Peace-maintenance has been defined by Jarat Chopra in his introduction as a concept that recognizes the need to exercise political authority by the international community in order to harmonize, and not merely coordinate, diplomatic, military, humanitarian, and other civilian components of peace operations. Civil administration, for the purposes of this article, relates to a number of the civilian functions in peace-maintenance. At one level, civilians may exercise executive powers of government, including direct control of ministries or varying degrees of support for their activities. At another, civilians may be involved in helping express the will of the people and developing civil society. This could include the supervision or organization and conduct of elections, as well as information management, including radio broadcasting. I argue that peace-maintenance is more likely to flourish if operations on the ground are both technically and politically appropriate, ideally based on the desire of the main parties to reach a solution; and if the main groups at the UN—now the West and the Nonaligned Movement—are ready not only to mandate the mission in question but also to ensure it continues to work on the right lines. In this sense, political legitimacy needs to be assured at both international and national levels.

In the UN context, political legitimacy for civil administration has depended primarily on the way states joining the organization and bound by its charter have sometimes been able to agree on certain intractable political issues, despite the fact they were part of the West, the East, or the Third World—represented by the Nonaligned Movement since 1961. This

41

explains why the UN has, for instance, deployed peacekeeping forces and monitored elections in trust territories seeking independence since 1956. International involvement in electoral matters was extended in the early 1960s to other colonial territories, after sixteen black African states joined the UN.[1] This occasional tripartite agreement also bore fruit in the human rights context, with the coming into force in 1976 of two covenants, on civil and political rights and on economic, social, and cultural rights. Furthermore, these three groupings—with the Nonaligned represented by Cyprus, Malta, and Yugoslavia—were all associated with the August 1975 Final Act of the Conference (now Organization) on Security and Cooperation in Europe. It has been argued that the Final Act really developed the concept of *internal* self-determination, or "the permanent possibility for a people to choose a new social or political regime, to adapt the social or political structure to meet new demands."[2]

The influence of this concept, among others, seems to have been one of the factors that led to the end of the Cold War, and with this, the disappearance of the East as a distinctive socialist alliance. In September 1991, the Nonaligned finally endorsed political pluralism at their foreign ministers' meeting in Accra. These changes meant that the interaction between the Nonaligned and the West, in the context of the legitimating structure of the UN Charter, remained a major key to achieving political legitimacy at an international level. An interface can exist here between power and justice.

The political legitimacy of operations on the ground has been strengthened since the end of the Cold War by the growing concern of the international community of states for the view of the people in a country. As a result, the UN monitors elections in *independent* countries, either as an integral part of a peace operation or in a separate mission mandated for the purpose; accounting for popular expression can add to the legitimacy of both the operation in question and the organization. While member states of the UN cannot wholly manufacture political will in the field, they can help strengthen it by ensuring that UN intervention is appropriately tailored to the political situation. As William Durch puts it, "A peacekeeping force derives its power from local consent, local perceptions of the impartiality and moral authority of its sponsoring organization, its ability to dispel dangerous misinformation, and the active support of the great powers."[3] It also needs the support of the Nonaligned majority in the General Assembly, who are represented in the Security Council.

It is worth examining the UN's overall involvement with civil administration against this background. The five examples of governmental civil administration discussed below are: the UN Operation in the Congo (ONUC); the UN Temporary Executive Authority (UNTEA) in West Irian; the UN Transition Assistance Group (UNTAG) in Namibia; the UN Mission for the Referendum in Western Sahara (MINURSO); and the UN Transitional Authority in Cambodia (UNTAC). In Chopra's terminology, they can be described, respectively, as: a mixture of *assistance, control,* and *governorship* in the Congo; *governorship* in West Irian; *partnership* in Namibia; *governorship* in Western Sahara; and *control* in Cambodia. The latter three are more connected with the organization of elections or referenda.

People's civil administration, in the form of electoral verification or assistance, is assessed in: the Second UN Angola Verification Mission (UNAVEM II); the UN Operation in Mozambique (ONUMOZ); and the UN Observer Mission in El Salvador (ONUSAL). These examples can be categorized as *assistance* in Angola and El Salvador, and *control* in Mozambique. Civil administration in the context of the former Yugoslavia has not been considered due to the shifting complexity of the situation.[4]

Cold War Dimensions of Civil Administration

UN involvement in civil administration of a governing kind goes back to 1947, when the Allied Powers agreed that the UN should ensure observance of the Permanent Statute for the Free Territory of Trieste. The territory was to be demilitarized and neutral, and a constitution was envisaged with a governor appointed by the Security Council. However, the council failed to agree on a governor; and the temporary arrangement of allied administration was kept in being until a final agreement was reached in 1954. The General Assembly also passed the partition resolution for Palestine in November 1947. Among other things, the member states called for a *corpus separatum* for the City of Jerusalem under a special international regime to be administered by the UN's Trusteeship Council, which would appoint a governor of the city; the governor would exercise all powers of administration including the conduct of external affairs. A draft statute for Jerusalem was prepared; it has not yet been used.

ONUC 1960–1964

The first peacekeeping, and subsequently peace-enforcement, operation in which certain civil administration tasks were integrated was that of ONUC in central Africa. One of its main functions was to assist the Congolese government to restore and maintain its territorial integrity and political independence, and to deal with other major problems of instability. As a result, the first chief of the UN civilian operation, responsible to the special representative of the secretary-general (SRSG), was appointed in July 1960. Specialized agencies were alerted and the UN International Children's Emergency Fund (UNICEF) set up an emergency food program, while steps were taken to clear the port of Matadi.

Complications were posed for the UN by the fact that the Congo was independent. In a memorandum of August 1960, the UN Secretary-General,

U Thant, noted that "the essential and long-term contribution [of the UN to the Congo] would be in the civilian field, but it required the establishment of order and security." Civilian activities were to be based on "the traditional pattern and methods of technical assistance . . . but they must go further," he added. "The United Nations must in the situation now facing the Congo go beyond the time-honoured forms of technical assistance in order to do what is necessary, *but it has to do it in forms which do not in any way infringe upon the sovereignty of the country or hamper the speedy development of the national administration . . . .*" The formula finally agreed upon made a distinction between technical assistance proper and "activities on a level of higher administrative responsibility, for which the experts employed must receive *a new and so far untried status.*" A consultative group was therefore attached to the chief of the UN civilian operation. Experts functioned as his consultants so they "would de facto be able to serve, with senior responsibility, at the request of the Government." The fields to be covered, mainly by specialized UN agencies, were: agriculture; communications; education; finance; foreign trade; health; instruction of national security forces; the labor market; the magistrature; natural resources and industry; and public administration.[5]

Experts were recruited in the first instance to restore or maintain minimum, essential public services, including monetary, foreign exchange, and foreign trade controls. The civilian operation was affected by the continuing constitutional crisis from September 1960 onward, which meant that "ONUC could not deal with any authorities, except for President Joseph Kasa-Vubu, on the nation-wide plane, and *could not furnish advice at the ministerial level.*" Nevertheless, it managed to continue to work "with those Congolese authorities exercising *de facto* control in the provinces or localities where United Nations Civilian Operations were being undertaken." And after the Katanga secession was brought to an end, civilian experts helped the central government to reintegrate the services previously under Katangese rule, including banking, civil aviation, customs and excise, immigration, postal services, and telecommunications.[6]

Overall, the civilian operations component employed some two thousand experts and technicians to help the Congolese government. U Thant noted in his final report that the UN had supplied personnel for some key economic and financial posts in the central administration:

> Four years have been gained in which the Government and people of the Congo have had the opportunity to come to grips with their vast problems and to be assisted in meeting some of the worst of them. Four years have been gained in which Congolese public administrators, doctors, professional people, experts of all kinds, and technicians could at least begin their training and begin to gain experience under the guidance and with the expert help of personnel of the United Nations and its specialized agencies.[7]

Information was as important a tool here as it proved in future operations. As early as mid-July 1960, the secretary-general's special representative in the Congo sent ONUC units to the radio and power stations of Léopoldville (now Kinshasa). In September, the new special representative closed the airport and radio station to all but the UN. This decision has remained the subject of great controversy.[8] Access to and control of the means, or some of the means, of information has proved crucial for peacekeeping and peace-enforcement.

It is difficult to assess the efficacy of this complex experiment given the constitutional problems against which UN officials had to operate. But civil administration seems, overall, to have contributed to the stability of the country.

UNTEA and UNSF 1962–1963

The status of the territory of West New Guinea (West Irian) had remained unresolved since Indonesian independence in 1949. The Dutch maintained that the Papuans should be allowed to decide their own future; the Indonesians asserted that West Irian was part of Indonesia. In 1961, the UN secretary-general began to use his good offices to resolve the problem. In September 1962, the General Assembly passed a resolution noting the Netherlands-Indonesian agreement that provided for the administration of West New Guinea to be transferred from the Netherlands to a UN temporary executive authority, after which the territory would be transferred to Indonesia. The secretary-general was asked to provide a UN security force (UNSF) to assist UNTEA. This was the first time the UN had assumed full administrative control of a territory.

The agreement provided for a UN administrator to conduct the actual transfer of authority over the territory. To do so, it gave UNTEA full powers to: appoint government officials and members of representative councils; legislate for the territory, subject to certain qualifications; and guarantee civil liberties and property rights. Some guarantees for the population of the territory were added, including UN participation in an act of self-determination to be held before the end of 1969.[9]

The commander of the UN security force, unlike many future force commanders, was responsible directly to the UN secretary-general. However, the force was an integral part of UNTEA and to that extent the military commander was also responsible to the civilian head in the field. UNTEA had to work through two stages after the security force had successfully supervised a cease-fire. First, Dutch civilian and military officials had to be phased out; then, Indonesian administrative personnel had to be phased in. The transition was supported by both Dutch and Indonesian radio stations.

The regions away from the operational headquarters in Hollandia (now Jayapura) were not neglected. In December 1962, the UNTEA administrator met members of the New Guinea Council and they took their new oath of office. They then returned to their constituencies to explain the new political situation. The administrator also specially requested divisional commissioners to consult the representative councils in their respective divisions on all important matters. Information policies were also devised. The UN administrator went on tour to explain the agreement. He was helped by a UN information campaign including news releases, publication of two periodicals, and daily broadcasts in English, Malay, and Dutch. One critique of the operation notes, however, that "regional information teams which were responsible for distributing news outside the major centers received no official instructions or material."[10] The acting special representative and the administrator also had to try to reactivate the judiciary, set up new regional councils, and deal with public information, news broadcasting, public health (including a cholera epidemic), education, and economic issues. The transfer was achieved peacefully.

Rosalyn Higgins observes that there were far fewer difficulties for UNTEA over consent and ambiguous mandates than there had been for ONUC and the UN Emergency Force (UNEF) in the Sinai. She notes that the time available to recruit and train personnel was too short, but points out that recruitment had begun provisionally some five weeks before the agreement was approved by the General Assembly. She accepts the argument in Paul van der Veur's critique on language difficulties, which states that "notably absent . . . was a core of experienced and neutral translators. The effects of complete ignorance of both Dutch and Malay/Indonesian can only be imagined." Higgins also concedes that goods moved to black markets, but she questions certain other assertions. Van der Veur's most serious criticism was that the smooth transfer was achieved at the cost of "the rights of free speech and assembly." Nevertheless, it seems clear that the UN enhanced its legitimacy on the ground by uneventfully passing power from the Netherlands to Indonesia.[11]

Post–Cold War Implications of Civil Administration

These reasonably efficacious Cold War missions set the stage for UNTAG, probably the most planned operation in UN history in terms of personnel and training. In both UNTEA and UNTAG, civilian directors reported to the special representative. And both operations showed, not surprisingly, that it was easier to work in the context of decolonization, in which agreements were implemented by the parties, than in an independent, sovereign country in the throes of civil war. The usefulness of a detailed mandate was demonstrated by UNTEA. Its two-part process may have paved the way for the stages decided on for UNTAG. Information dissemination and contacts with the regions away from a capital city have been a consistent concern of those involved with civil administration. Each operation helped resolve a difficult and complex situation through the legitimation provided by the UN, which afforded them at least partial acceptance on the ground.

UNTAG 1989–1990

Security Council Resolution 435 of 1978, authorizing a UN transition assistance group to ensure the early independence of Namibia, was finally implemented after a further resolution in February 1989. Momentum came from the indispensable credibility provided by a U.S. decision "in 1981 to operate within a U.N. framework and to retain Resolution 435 as the basis and pivot for a settlement."[12] The resolution of the Namibia problem, as I have argued elsewhere, proved possible because it was undertaken in the context of the legitimacy provided by a UN framework.[13]

UNTAG's mandate covered: military supervision of the cease-fire; monitoring existing security forces; creating the conditions for free and fair elections; organizing the return of refugees; and finally, supervising and controlling South Africa's conduct of the election for an assembly that would draft Namibia's constitution.[14] Martti Ahtisaari, the SRSG for Namibia from mid-1978, later noted, "We not only had to monitor and try to prevent violence but also had to establish UNTAG as *a legitimate authority*—in all its components—throughout the territory. This meant gaining the trust of the people by being seen to act with discretion and integrity, and in particular be known as a source of objective information (something that the country had been starved of for years)." He pointed out that (unlike his counterparts in Cambodia and Western Sahara, for example) he was in charge of the mission's planning and, subsequently, "in the run-up to implementation in 1988 . . . was under-secretary-general [of the UN] for administration and management." He was therefore able to release appropriate staff and train them for the operation, neither of which had been done before.[15]

Despite these advantages, UNTAG became fully operational two months late, in May 1989, because of budget difficulties. At maximum deployment, it had thirty-five hundred civilians, including fifteen hundred civilian police (CIVPOL). The South African administrator-general was enjoined, from the beginning, to ensure a number of acts took place before the election campaign began, including the repeal of all remaining discriminatory or restrictive laws. All these conditions had to be fulfilled to the satisfaction of the special representative. This ratcheting occurred at each stage of the political process. A further aid to its smooth working was the establishment of a joint working group on all aspects of impartiality. Set up early in the proceedings to deal with the many minor but aggravating political problems, it met weekly.

The network of district political offices was also extremely important. As Ingrid Lehmann has noted, their "job was to report to the . . . [SRSG] about political developments in their districts" and "inform the population as to the nature of UNTAG's mandate, the purposes of the UN peace plan . . . and the reasons for the UN presence in their country." Its main difficulty was "that the UNTAG district structure did not match the South African administrative structure."[16] Ahtisaari adds that "the civilian component was also responsible for overall coordination, within region or district, of the UN components. In a multi-functional mission, so broadly dispersed geographically, with each component reporting vertically to its central headquarters, the danger of non-communication and confusion is ever present. Habitually, there can be major problems of lateral contact, at every level. . . . In the light of the experience of UNTAG, both coordination and teamwork cannot be stressed too strongly as the basis of any successful mission. Without these two, confusion, waste of resources, and a diffused effectiveness are the consequence."[17]

According to Cedric Thornberry, the civilian chief-of-staff in Namibia, "UNTAG's credibility depended very much on its visibility, operational effectiveness, and *legitimacy* in the eyes of the population. Much propaganda over many years had been aimed at portraying the UN as favouring one Namibian political party only," the South West Africa People's Organization (SWAPO). Combating this view was one of the functions of UNTAG's regional and district staff, who were responsible for public information and liaison coordination between the components of UNTAG, as well as administrative and general matters. "They were the eyes and ears—and voice—of UNTAG throughout the country, charged with creating a new atmosphere and climate of reconciliation. It had been intrinsic to UNTAG's strategic planning from its earliest conception that such steps would be taken by it as would lead, during the transition period, to the growth of a spirit of tolerance and democratic participation. . . . By the time of the election many UNTAG offices had developed an unofficial 'ombudsman' role as regards political and related human rights' issues."[18] This process was helped by regular all-party meetings, to resolve such problems as harassment of party workers. They were held throughout the territory in the context of a code of conduct for political parties, which had been developed in July 1989.

One reason for the success of this campaign was the use of creative methods and information material in eleven languages to educate the population for voter registration and the elections. District political officers held meetings with community leaders and trade union officials, and gained access at all levels to farms. Once again, the use of radio was an important issue. Lehmann argues that "during the election, UNTAG radio communications became really the one and only, the exclusive channel of communications functioning throughout the country. In my district, we gave South African officials access to our radios, which allowed us to straighten out any problems at any polling station on very short notice."[19] She also noted the importance of training on the ground and the use of racially mixed registration and polling teams.

Something of a peace-maintenance framework and its political legitimacy became possible, according to Marrack Goulding, then UN under secretary-general for special political affairs, because of the "continuing support of the members of the Security Council and other interested states [such as the Nonaligned Movement and the African group] during the implementation of the operation."[20] This enhanced the overall success of the operation on the ground.

MINURSO 1991–

MINURSO was the result of a joint peace-making effort by the UN secretary-general and the Organization of African Unity (OAU). The so-called settlement plan was to resolve the long-standing dispute between Morocco and the Popular Front for the Liberation of Saguia el-Hamra and of Rio de Oro (POLISARIO) about the status of Western Sahara. In 1988, the two parties agreed in principle to implement the plan through a UN referendum mission. After a problematic planning period, MINURSO was authorized by the Security Council in April 1991. In the first instance, the mission was supposed to determine when the transition period, beginning with a cease-fire, was to come into effect. Voter lists were to be closed before this date, which was also to coincide with cantonment of combatants (then a new area for the UN) and the publication of consolidated voters' lists. Local laws contrary to a free and fair election were subsequently to be suspended and the referendum held, followed by the withdrawal of the loser.

In fact, the transition period never formally began. The cease-fire of September 1991 was effectively divorced from it. In May 1996, the UN secretary-general noted that the original settlement plan had provided for "close linkage between the cease-fire and the political process," but by the autumn of 1995 there were "irreconcilable differences between the parties" about the identification of voter applicants.[21] He concluded that conditions did not exist for a free and fair referendum, and proposed cancellation of identification and a reduction in strength of MINURSO, though not its withdrawal.

One observer stated in 1993 that "the entire enterprise suffered from a fundamental unresolved problem: although both local parties were prepared to submit their dispute to a referendum, neither side was prepared to lose."[22] Potential losers need a stake in the future. And the international community is still too divided to provide much leverage on the internal situation in the context of a joint-contact group of friends of Western

Sahara.[23] On both the international and national level, it appears that legitimacy was lacking.

UNTAC 1992–1993

The conflict in independent Cambodia, exacerbated by Sino-Soviet differences, had long been a focus of UN diplomatic efforts. Attempts to make peace were renewed at the Paris Conference on Cambodia in 1989 and continued by the permanent members of the Security Council in 1990. They suggested that UNTAC would control five key ministries and accepted that the rival governments could continue to exist, but under supervision, to try to ensure a neutral political environment for elections. The Cambodian parties, including the Party of Democratic Kampuchea (PDK) representing the Khmer Rouge, accepted the plan in August 1990. In September, Security Council members welcomed the agreement of the four factions to form the Supreme National Council (SNC) as the "unique legitimate body and source of authority in which throughout the transitional period the sovereignty, independence and unity of Cambodia . . . [would be] embodied."

UNTAC was finally established in February 1992. Its complex mandate included seven components: human rights, electoral, military, civil administration, police, repatriation, and rehabilitation. But already there were problems concerning legitimacy. According to the military force commander of UNTAC, Lt. Gen. John Sanderson, "the corruption of the peace process began in Phnom Penh" in November 1991, "firstly when Prince Sihanouk, on his return, attempted to form an alliance between his son . . . the royalist party leader and . . . the SOC [State of Cambodia] prime minister; and secondly when the Khmer Rouge were run out of the city on 27 November 1991, following a series of clearly orchestrated demonstrations."[24]

UNTAC was supposed to achieve "a comprehensive settlement" in Cambodia, giving special attention to foreign affairs, national defense, finance, public security, and information. It was authorized to "exercise such control as is necessary to ensure the strict neutrality of the bodies responsible for them."[25] Lyndall McLean points out that one major problem was the failure to translate into Khmer the secretary-general's report of February 1992, which contained the proposed implementation plan.[26] Regarding civil administration, this blueprint noted that the UN would use codes of conduct and guidelines for management; it would scrutinize areas such as passports and visas, military expenditure, control over planning (including allocation of resources and budgeting), banking, customs, human rights (including effective redress of grievances), and information; and finally, it would establish the critical complaints and investigation service within civil administration channels.

In addition, other problems plagued UNTAC. Only 170 staff were assigned to civil administration activities for twenty-one provinces and a central administration. Information officers were not sent to each province as planned. Inexperienced staff were recruited. It suffered from too little cooperation between different components and from a dismal shortage of Khmer interpreters. Few of its guidelines were finalized. And there were too many abuses by political parties of civil administration—including the prevention of assembly and intrusion into political party meetings. To address the shortcomings, UNTAC civil administrators set up a complaints clarification committee for the police and human rights components; it could issue restraining orders in such disputes as those about property claims. They also ensured that provincial governors and city mayors issued directives to district offices about their responsibilities for the peace process, and that a memorandum of understanding was reached with provincial authorities about what information UNTAC needed. Finally, they convened regular roundtable meetings with the political parties.

McLean suggests that the greatest failure of the civil administration component concerned corrective action or redress. A "lack of political will combined with . . . legal difficulties . . . prevented the UN from ever bringing alleged wrongdoers to prosecution." Nor were suitable financial controls instituted. Some success could be recorded in the area of public information, as UNTAC eventually "negotiated access to print shops for the production of party materials" and opposition parties got access to UNTAC radio and television. McLean notes this should have been established earlier—since it was not set up until October 1992—and used to draw attention to actions of noncompliance with the Paris Agreement.[27] However, she argues, the crucial areas were ultimately public security, civic education, and information.

Electoral planning based on the Namibian experience was a success—although in Cambodia the UN had full responsibility for the conduct of the poll, unlike the partnership arrangement in Namibia.[28] One factor seems to have been the critical support provided by the military component of UNTAC, including their supervision of ballot boxes. That ballot papers from individual stations were mixed with those from at least two others also helped to ensure secret voting. Cambodians appreciated and trusted the secrecy promised by UNTAC's information campaign sufficiently to turn out on election day, despite extensive intimidation throughout the country in late 1992 and early 1993.

Much has already been published about this operation.[29] Michael Doyle, in his fascinating study, draws attention to the need for a combination of local, regional, and international support, and a multidimensional mandate. UNTAC failed when the parties were not willing to cooperate. Passive support was the minimum needed. UNTAC was more likely to succeed when actions "taken by or directly organized by" it "did not require the positive cooperation of the four factions to be effective."[30] But this depended on its being able to sell itself to the local population, the other major actor—which it did. Ultimately, the legitimacy of UNTAC's electoral side seems to have been undermined by insufficient legitimacy on its governmental side, which the lack of genuine agreement between the main political parties had subverted.

UNAVEM II 1991–1995 and ONUMOZ 1992–1994

UNAVEM II and ONUMOZ were both set up to help resolve civil wars in former Portuguese colonies. I discuss these operations together, since lessons learned from the resumption of civil war after the election in the former helped ensure the latter's success. In May 1991, the Security Council authorized UNAVEM II to monitor the implementation of the peace accords that had just been agreed, without much UN input, between the Angolan government and the National Union for the Total Independence of Angola (UNITA). The process was to culminate in an election, which was eventually held in September 1992. The Security Council subsequently endorsed the view of the SRSG that the elections were "generally free and fair." UNITA, however, did not agree, and civil war resumed.

The Special Representative, Margaret Anstee, has commented that "the elections went off exceedingly well" because of the longing for peace of the Angolan people, as well as the work of the multiparty national election council and the director-general of the elections. The UN had a mandate, however, only to observe and verify the elections with a limited number of election observers—eventually four hundred. Angola, with an electorate six times that of Namibia, received one thousand UN international personnel in all, in contrast to the eight thousand provided for Namibia. Once again, as in Western Sahara, an inappropriate political structure hampered those preparing the elections. Neither the expected demobilization and disarmament of each side's army nor the formation of the new army had taken place. The implementation of the accords was put into jeopardy because the parties—not Boy Scouts, as Anstee points out—had each been given sole responsibility in this area.[31] The position of the special representative was just as a guest in the top joint-monitoring mechanism. Even more important, perhaps, few incentives had been built in for the election's loser. Mediation after the results focused on this problem. As in both Western Sahara and (to some extent) Cambodia, there was insufficient agreement on the ground for political legitimacy to be achieved. Nevertheless, more might have been accomplished if the operation had been given more attention.

Many lessons learned in Angola were corrected for its ex-Portuguese sister colony, Mozambique. First, the timetable was more rigorously adhered to. The assembly and demobilization of both armies was almost complete before the elections and the training of new armed forces had begun. Second, a compromise was reached about control of the parties in their respective provinces. Third, flexibility was allowed: the elections were postponed when it became apparent that the first phase needed more time to stay on course. Fourth, SRSG Aldo Ajello was given more authority than Anstee. Ajello chaired the top body: the supervisory and monitoring commission. Finally, incentives were built in for both parties, not just for the one that prevailed in the elections.[32]

The elections appear to have been technically well prepared. Ensuring the viability of the political structure within which they were organized led to their success and legitimacy. Uncharacteristic of UN operations, this was not the end of the process. Now, following the centerpiece election, much thinking focuses on the question of how basic human security can be achieved through "access to food, shelter and health."[33]

ONUSAL 1991–1995

On 15 December 1992, the armed conflict was formally brought to an end between the El Salvador government and the Farabundo Martí National Liberation Front (FMLN), which was to become a legalized political party through the peace process. ONUSAL had become operational in July 1991, to verify and implement a number of agreements adopted by the two parties between 1990 and early 1992. Its supervisory role was expanded in November 1993 to include observation of the 1994 elections. The scope of the process was extremely ambitious. It aimed at "nothing less than eliminating the cause of the conflict: a militarized society, riven by profound economic and social inequalities and a closed political system."[34]

ONUSAL's original three divisions covered human rights, police, and the military. Its electoral division began to operate in September 1993, to support voter registration and oversee the electoral campaign and polling. Successful elections were held in April 1994.[35] The major problems, noted in the secretary-general's final and preceding reports, included organization of elections, the proper preparation of an electoral roll, and the "evident need for a thorough reform of the electoral system." The UN remained "ready to provide technical support in connection with such a reform, which should include as key elements a single identity document, provision for voting in the area of residence of the voter, standardization of the formula for representation in the Assembly and municipalities, and depoliticization of the Supreme Electoral Tribunal."[36]

A further concern, as Alvaro de Soto and Graciana del Castillo point out, was that:

> [the] elections deflected attention from the peace process and politicized it at the same time. They also induced a false analogy with Cambodia,

where, in accordance with the Paris agreement, the holding of elections and the establishment of a new government largely concluded the UN's peacekeeping involvement. Such a schedule was never intended for El Salvador. . . . The issue that arises now is how to move away from a peacekeeping operation *stricto sensu*—i.e., one involving military and police personnel—to an operation in which the UN can continue discharging its verification and good offices responsibilities, without losing the momentum provided by pressure from the international community through the . . . [Security Council], and in doing so how to harness the programs and agencies of the UN system so that they work toward the same goal of peace consolidation.[37]

Once the mission was concluded in April 1995, the secretary-general set up a small political office for six months, a mechanism to continue ONUSAL's verification responsibilities and good offices function.[38] Its purpose was to enable him to alert the council if problems arose, and to provide guidance to the UN Development Programme (UNDP). The basic ingredients for political legitimacy seem to have been met. Time will tell if the results are lasting.

Requirements and Evolution of Peace-Maintenance

This chapter concentrates on peacekeeping and peace-enforcement operations that have had one or all of the following dimensions of civil administration: involvement with government ministries; election verification, assistance, or organization; and aspects of information management. Five of the eight case studies relate to independent countries—the Congo, Cambodia, Angola, Mozambique, and El Salvador. The other three—West Irian, Namibia, and Western Sahara—remain of interest, despite the fact that each mission was assigned to change the status of a nonindependent territory.

Certain technical and political conclusions drawn from these experiences are set out in the following section. It also considers how international and national political legitimacy in peace-maintenance can be achieved—to complement Clement Adibe's chapter about inclusion of the local population—and, finally, how this is most likely to evolve in the next few years.

Technical and Political Lessons

The eight case studies indicate that the following technical and political elements need to be considered within the context of a legitimate peace-maintenance framework (discussed in the next section). Many of these requirements, not surprisingly, transcend the specifics of civil administration.

Lesson 1. Good consistent planning and appropriate training for personnel, including civilians for a range of jobs, need to be combined with a coherent mandate that is supported by both the West and the Nonaligned. The usefulness of good planning was particularly noticeable in Namibia.

Lesson 2. The danger of committing UN personnel in too marginal a way was notable in UNAVEM II. There can be overreliance on a best-case-scenario outcome, in which the initial agreement between the two parties is expected to be implemented willingly on the ground. Although every mission has an element of risk, assessment of the readiness of the parties to move forward and of their stake in the outcome needs to be done *before* the operation takes place. Sanctions that could be imposed if necessary ought to be factored into any settlement equation. New techniques can be tried to foster the parties' adherence to the terms they endorse. For instance, the usefulness of radio to draw attention to noncompliance with the original agreement or accepted guidelines was illustrated in the context of UNTAC.

Lesson 3. UN member states must try to ensure that respect for the organization and its principles continues to be a cornerstone of any agreement, guidelines, joint monitoring commission, or other arrangement. And its personnel should reflect this in their adherence to appropriate codes of conduct, which need to be developed. States can not use the UN's powers of legitimation for ends contrary to the charter. However, although state sovereignty has to be respected, the UN leadership on the ground needs to be aware of the areas in which it can take the initiative, as illustrated in Mark Plunkett's chapter, which follows. These are areas in which the consent of the parties needs only to be passive.

Lesson 4. Sufficient resources have to be made available if an operation is to function. The timing of their delivery is also important. The amount of resources available for Angola compared to those given to Namibia may well have determined the result. Allowing the SRSG, or the Security Council, in Namibia and Mozambique the ability to *delay* aspects of the peace plan until other parts of the operation had been completed proved a useful practice.

Lesson 5. Effective measures to spread information remain indispensable.[39] In each case discussed above, a number of media were used to spread the UN message among the population of the country concerned. These need to be refined and adapted specifically to each operation. In this context, it is important to provide missions in places with uncommon languages, as in West Irian or Cambodia, with sufficient interpreters and translated material.

Lesson 6. The use of joint mechanisms as higher courts of appeal that can hear complaints on a variety of levels has proved its worth, particularly in Namibia. Their experience should be assessed to make them work better and in a more lasting way in the future.

Lesson 7. The relationship between those deployed in provinces and those in the capital needs to be better integrated. Separate components of multifunctional missions having to cooperate with each other at the provincial level but reporting independently to their own headquarters is a problem to be addressed. This will affect the numbers of civilians to be deployed as well as their chains of command. Peace planners also need to carefully consider flexible ways of relating to local government (if it exists) and nongovernmental organizations. They may need to rebuild local government and will have to be prepared appropriately, as Andy Knight has already described.

Lesson 8. The UN (and others) have developed effective methods of election verification, assistance, and organization. These need to be further developed to guarantee that the whole population in the countries concerned continues to have a stake in nonviolent methods of political change.

Lesson 9. Finally, the case studies above suggest that the UN has been more successful overall in the electoral exercises of people's civil administration than in governmental civil administration. The latter has worked best in nonindependent territories—in West Irian and Namibia, although not in Western Sahara. It was less effective in the Congo and Cambodia.

Some of these lessons have been applied in Latin American countries like Guatemala. In May 1996, the Agreement on Social and Economic Aspects and the Agrarian Situation was concluded between the Guatemalan government and the Unidad Revolucionaria Nacional Guatemalteca (URNG) Command. It was signed in the presence of members of the Group of Friends of the Guatemalan Peace Process, comprising Colombia—the current chair of the Nonaligned Movement; Mexico; Norway; Spain; the United States; and Venezuela. As the UN secretary-general notes, "At the heart of the strategies outlined in the agreement is the concept, consistent with the thinking of the United Nations, that enhanced social participation in all aspects of development is key to both improved social justice and sustainable economic growth."[40] The agreement does not include the deployment of UN military contingents, but it is worth mentioning here in a political context.

Achieving Political Legitimacy

The link between certain UN resolutions and legitimacy was asserted by Chester A. Crocker in the context of the Namibian settlement. But as

Anthony Parsons wrote in 1995, "in foreign policy decision making, disinterested internationalism is coming a very poor second to national interest in a world of proliferating civil conflicts far from major power centres; except when public outrage demands action, and the prospect of unpopularity through inactivity looms."[41] Nevertheless, the connection holds as a kind of global consensus emerges. The Western states and the Nonaligned continue to proclaim their commitment to UN principles—and, more and more, they adhere to the major human rights covenants.[42] In particular circumstances, noted in the introduction to this chapter, they have agreed on intractable political issues. The five most recent peace operations discussed above were all approved by unanimous Security Council resolutions. The earlier three were not. Peace-maintenance should not be fostered without this kind of framework.

However, authoritative resolutions are not always enough. Support groups, consisting mostly of interested states (often called "friends of" the country or territory in question) have at times been created to ensure the peace-making process continues throughout implementation. The importance of such support in the Namibia case and in Guatemala has already been noted, as has its fatal absence in Western Sahara. Similar bodies existed for Cambodia and El Salvador. That none was organized for Angola may have been significant. Furthermore, the five permanent members of the Security Council have often acted together as a group on similar issues since the mid-1980s.[43] Achieving political legitimacy by such means is threatened, however, by the fact that some permanent members and other states are in arrears with their UN contributions.

At the national level, peace-maintenance operations will work best when they have moral authority, appropriate organization, and an ability to provide information, and when, in addition, they are impartial and supported by the local community. Missions tend not to succeed when these conditions are absent, as the examples of Western Sahara and Angola show.

The Future

The current questioning of the UN has had an effect on the rate of establishing new peace operations. This slower pace will probably continue in the near future. And pressures for UN, including Security Council, reform have not yet reached any conclusion. Given these factors, it seems unlikely that the way legitimacy is achieved in peace operations, either on the ground or internationally, is going to change substantially. Joint frameworks will therefore need to be adapted and strengthened if UN resolutions are to be successfully implemented in peace-maintenance.

Although UN members found governmental civil administration in independent countries more difficult than assisting in popular elections, excessive reliance on the ballot box has in turn raised new questions, such as in Cambodia and El Salvador. That is, the emphasis is perhaps beginning to shift from concentration on a single electoral event to a discussion of how this fits into the development of civil society. Responding to this in the next few years may be the principal challenge in achieving the political legitimacy of effective peace-maintenance. ⊕

Notes

Sally Morphet is a research analyst and head of the Global Issues Research Group at the British Foreign and Commonwealth Office. She has published a number of articles and chapters in books on human rights, the Nonaligned, peacekeeping and the Security Council. The opinions expressed are the author's own and should not be taken as an expression of official British government policy.

1. See the useful "Secretary-General's Report on Enhancing the Effectiveness of the Principle of Periodic and Genuine Elections," UN. Doc. A/46/609 of 19 November 1991. This lists the thirty-two plebiscites, referenda, and elections held under the supervision or observation of the UN in trust and non-self-governing territories between 1956 and 1990. Only the Namibian elections were held as an integral part of a larger peace operation.

2. See Sally Morphet, "Article 1 of the Human Rights Covenants: Its Development and Current Significance in Human Rights and Foreign Policy," in Dilys Hill, ed., *Economic, Social and Cultural Rights: Progress and Achievement* (London: Macmillan, 1989), pp. 81–82.

3. William J. Durch, "Building on Sand: UN Peacekeeping in the Western Sahara," *International Security* 17, no. 4 (spring 1993): 153.

4. Although, see the useful article by Cedric Thornberry, EYEWITNESS II, "Civil Affairs in the Development of UN Peacekeeping," *International Peacekeeping* 1, no. 4 (winter 1994): 471–484.

5. See Rosalyn Higgins, *Africa*, vol. 3 of *United Nations Peacekeeping 1946–1967, Documents and Commentary* (Oxford: Oxford University Press, 1980), pp. 77–80 (italics added).

6. See UN, *The Blue Helmets: A Review of United Nations Peacekeeping*, 2d ed. (New York: United Nations Department of Public Information, 1990), pp. 253–256 (italics added).

7. See Higgins, *Africa*, pp. 364–378, especially p. 376.

8. Ibid., pp. 304, 144–148. See also Georges Abi-Saab, *The United Nations Operation in the Congo, 1960–1964* (Oxford: Oxford University Press, 1978), pp. 59–75.

9. On the agreement, see Rosalyn Higgins, *Asia*, vol. 2 of *United Nations Peacekeeping 1946–1967, Documents and Commentary* (Oxford: Oxford University Press, 1970), pp. 101–106.

10. Paul W. van der Veur, "The United Nations in West New Guinea: a Critique," *International Organization* 18, no. 1 (winter 1964): 61.

11. See Higgins, *Asia*, pp. 128, 141–142; van der Veur, "West New Guinea": 59, 71.

12. Chester A. Crocker, *High Noon in Southern Africa: Making Peace in a Rough Neighbourhood* (New York: W. W. Norton, 1992), pp. 454–455.

13. See Sally Morphet, "Resolutions and vetoes in the UN Security Council: their relevance and significance," *Review of International Studies* 16, no. 4 (October 1990): 357–358.

14. Compare Marrack Goulding and Ingrid Lehmann, "Case Study: The United Nations Operation in Namibia," in UN, *The Singapore Symposium: The Changing Role of the United Nations in Conflict Resolution and Peace-Keeping, 13–15 March 1991* (New York: United Nations Department of Public Information, 1991), pp. 33–41.

15. Heribert Weiland and Matthew Braham, Rapporteurs of the Freiburg Symposium, July 1992, *The Namibian Peace Process: Implications and Lessons for the Future* (Freiburg: Arnold Bergstraesser Institut/International Peace Academy, 1994), pp. 61–62 (italics added).

16. UN, *Singapore Symposium*, pp. 35–36.

17. Weiland and Braham, *Namibian Peace Process*, p. 64.

18. Cedric Thornberry, "UNTAG: Description and Analysis of the Mission's Operational Arrangements," September 1991, manuscript, pp. 50, 55 (italics added).

19. UN, *Singapore Symposium*, p. 36.

20. Ibid., p. 38.

21. UN Doc. S/1996/343 of 8 May 1996.

22. Durch, "Building on Sand," p. 160.

23. See the proposal by Jarat Chopra, "A Chance for Peace in Western Sahara," *Survival* 39, no. 3 (autumn 1997): 51–65.

24. Lt. Gen. J. M. Sanderson, "UNTAC: Successes and Failures," in Hugh Smith, ed., *International Peacekeeping: Building on the Cambodian Experience* (Canberra: Australian Defence Studies Centre, 1994), p. 18.

25. Based on Lyndall McLean, "Civil Administration in Transition: Public Information and the Neutral Political/Electoral Environment," in Smith, *Cambodian Experience*, pp. 47–58.

26. UN Doc. S/23613 and Addendum I of 19 February 1992.

27. McLean, "Civil Administration in Transition," pp. 55–56.

28. See Michael Maley, "Reflections on the Electoral Process in Cambodia," in Hugh Smith, ed., *Peacekeeping: Challenges for the Future* (Canberra: Australian Defence Studies Centre, 1993), pp. 87–99.

29. See the interesting studies in Trevor Findlay, *Cambodia: The Legacy and Lessons of UNTAC* (Oxford: Stockholm International Peace Research Institute/Oxford University Press, 1995); Michael W. Doyle, *UN Peacekeeping in Cambodia: UNTAC's Civil Mandate* (Boulder: International Peace Academy/Lynne Rienner, 1995).

30. Doyle, *UNTAC's Civil Mandate*, pp. 59–71.

31. Margaret J. Anstee, "Angola: The Forgotten Tragedy—A Test Case for U.N. Peacekeeping," *International Relations* 11, no. 6 (December 1993): 495, 497; generally 495–500. See also Anstee, *Orphan of the Cold War: The Inside Story of the Collapse of the Angolan Peace Process, 1992–1993* (New York: St. Martin's Press, 1996).

32. See Chris Alden, "The UN and the Resolution of Conflict in Mozambique," *Journal of Modern African Studies*, 33, no. 1 (March 1995): 103–128.

33. See Susan Willett, "Ostriches, Wise Old Elephants and Economic Reconstruction in Mozambique," *International Peacekeeping* 2, no. 1 (spring 1995): 34–55.

34. See Alvaro de Soto and Graciana del Castillo, "Implementation of Comprehensive Peace Agreements: Staying the Course in El Salvador," *Global Governance* 1, no. 2 (May-August 1995): 189.

35. See UN Doc. S/1995/144, in UN, *The United Nations and El Salvador, 1990–1995*, UN Blue Book Series, vol. 4 (New York: United Nations Department

of Public Information, 1995), pp. 491–493, 505–506, 521–535, 542–547. See also Alexandre S. Kamaratos, "Building Peace, Democracy and Human Rights: International Civilian Missions at the End of the Millennium," *International Peacekeeping* 2, no. 4 (winter 1995): 483–509.

36. See UN Doc. S/1994/536, in UN, *The United Nations and El Salvador*, pp. 546–547.

37. See de Soto and del Castillo, "Comprehensive Peace Agreements," pp. 190–191.

38. See UN, *The United Nations and El Salvador*, pp. 598–599.

39. See for instance, Peter Loizos, with Gordon Adam and Jelena Subotic, "Broadcasting for Restraint: Crisis Reduction Through UN-Supported Media Initiatives," in Anthony McDermott, ed., *Ethnic Conflict and International Security* (Oslo: Norwegian Institute of International Affairs, 1994), pp. 89–102.

40. See "Letter from the UN Secretary-General to the President of the General Assembly," UN Doc. A/50/956 of 6 June 1996, p. 1.

41. Anthony Parsons, *From Cold War to Hot Peace: UN Interventions 1947–1995* (London: Penguin, 1995), p. 270.

42. See Sally Morphet, "The Non-Aligned in 'The New World Order': The Jakarta Summit, September 1992," *International Relations* 11, no. 4 (April 1993): 359–380.

43. See Sally Morphet, "The influence of states and groups of states on and in the Security Council and General Assembly, 1980–1994," *Review of International Studies* 21, no. 4 (October 1995): 444–445, 452–453.

4

Reestablishing Law and Order in Peace-Maintenance

—————— ⊕ ——————

Mark Plunkett

D
emand for UN intervention around the globe has been extraordinary since the end of the Cold War. As a result, the 1990s have witnessed the greatest number of peace operations in the UN's five decades. Most have been ambitious in scope and often muddled in execution, particularly in Somalia, Cambodia, and the former Yugoslavia. Unprecedented difficulties emerged for the UN as circumstances required it to expand its role in the field. It increasingly had to undertake many onerous tasks for the first time and without any prior experience. This chapter sets out, for scholars and future policymakers and planners, the issues that have arisen and that require urgent consideration in the justice area of peace-maintenance. It does so fundamentally through the case history of Cambodia, but distills the requirements of success for the kinds of civilian missions described above in Sally Morphet's chapter.

As states collapse, the former surrogate nations can no longer look to their previous sponsors for humanitarian, economic, and military assistance. The end of the twentieth century has witnessed the disintegration of the strategic balance between two antagonistic superpowers that divided the world into rival ideological and political camps for nearly half a century after World War II. Russia and the independent remnants of the Soviet Union survive with few resources. And the United States, it seems, undergoes periodic, protracted domestic debate about whether to embark on international undertakings with the UN when asked to do so by world opinion driven, from time to time, by mass media attention.

Unfortunately, new crises continue to erupt in multiple regions, spontaneously and without warning. The UN, asked to intervene again and again, will turn to domestically stable and reasonably wealthy member countries for help. The main institution called upon for short-term security in peace operations has been the military; but increasingly now civilian police (CIVPOL) and legal experts are needed to establish in the longer term a rule of law.

Reestablishing Law and Order

Past UN peacekeeping and peace-enforcing missions have included civilian personnel in various operational phases but were designed to rely mostly on the military. This is because at every stage of a crisis (including graduation into postconflict resolution and reconstruction), life-threatening disorder requires the deployment in the field of a significant force of armed, disciplined, and trained units to deter and contend with violence, together with associated logistical support of rapid transport and communications, which only the military possess.

As a result of the second generation of peace experiments outlined in Jarat Chopra's introduction, however, a pattern is currently emerging of relative civil-military tasks. It begins with the military and—as a crisis deescalates—gradually increases the role of civilians, as follows:

1. Rescue of international persons
2. Security and protection of UN civilian personnel and nongovernmental organizations (NGOs) in international humanitarian assistance
3. Security and protection of refugees and noncombatants in areas of "safe haven"
4. Detection, investigation, and prosecution of war crimes and crimes of genocide
5. Initiation and mediation of cease-fire agreements
6. Observing and monitoring cease-fire agreements
7. Organization and facilitation of a transition to peace through: (a) the disarming, demobilization, and cantonment of the armies of factions; (b) the creation of a neutral political environment, including: the development and implementation of a program of human rights education, to promote respect for and understanding of human rights; general human rights oversight during the transitional period; the investigation of human rights complaints; and, where appropriate, the taking of corrective action; (c) the holding of free and fair elections; (d) the election of a democratic government; (e) the rebuilding of executive infrastructure; and (f) the reestablishment of the rule of law

This chapter is principally concerned with one element of the list: the critical place of human rights lawyers and CIVPOL in all phases of peace-maintenance, and especially in the postconflict stage of a crisis. Justice professionals in such contexts have three primary, paralleled functions: (1) the detection, investigation, and prosecution of war crimes and crimes of genocide; (2) human rights observance, education, and correction; and (3) the reestablishment of the rule of law. The specific dimensions of each are detailed in the latter part of the chapter.

All three tasks are challenging and ranked in ascending degree of complexity and difficulty. The first concerns prosecution in all geographic areas of the conflict. What is apparent from recent experience in peace operations is the increasing need for cooperation between international troops, lawyers, and CIVPOL in the detection, investigation, and prosecution of war crimes and crimes of genocide. A combined effort is required at all stages of the crisis and continues well after the transition to peace. The second task is required at all times in areas under UN control, and especially during the transition to peace, to engender the neutral political environment necessary for a free and fair election. The third task, the reestablishment of the rule of law, is reserved invariably for the postconflict stage. But, as in all of the recent UN peace missions—not just in Cambodia, but in places like Bosnia, Angola, and Western Sahara—the lines are blurred between when the war ends and the peace begins. Justice officials will inevitably find themselves in a similarly grey area.

The experience of lawyers and CIVPOL in these three tasks is essentially of recent origin, and dates from the UN's 1989 deployment in Namibia.[1] Perhaps the only other historic parallels have been the war crimes trials and nation rebuilding in Europe and Asia following World War II, and the decolonization process in Africa and generally. Despite their diversity of national origins and variety of jurisdictions, UN lawyers and CIVPOL share an uncanny unanimity in their professional standards, requirements, and manner of undertaking these tasks. UN hierarchies have failed them, however, by a regrettable dearth of understanding. Until now, each activity has been approached reactively and incrementally. There are many lessons to be learned from recent mistakes. After nearly a decade, the combined corporate knowledge of lawyers and police serving in UN peace missions has reached the point where it is time to pause to reflect on proper planning principles and policies for justice in peace-maintenance.

The ultimate objective of peace operations has been the conclusion or implementation of a negotiated agreement and the holding of elections. These priorities have been the engines driving most missions. The emphasis has been on the formation of a legitimate, internationally recognized government, on which is usually made contingent international aid through the UN, the World Bank, and national capitals. Specifically, attention is focused on the creation of an executive branch through a democratically elected legislature. In turn, there has been insufficient regard by UN planners for the reestablishment of an underlying rule of law. Peace without justice is likely to result in a breach birth for a new nation. A young democracy without an established rule of law may soon degenerate into a people ruled by warlords and tribalism. A fragile government without an independent and adequately resourced judiciary may soon perish. Certainly, only after the cessation of hostilities can law and order be expected, but a lasting peace is not achievable unless it carries with it the imperative of law. Recent peacekeeping and peace-enforcing experiences have indicated, therefore, that the most fundamental requirement, and a primary objective, of a lasting peace is the reestablishment of the rule of law.

The Cambodian Experience

It is instructive to conduct a postmission audit years after a peace operation to determine the effectiveness or otherwise of the intervention. For example, the most serious threat to the democratically elected government in Cambodia since 1993 has been more the unabated corruption of its leaders at the national and provincial level, through to general lawlessness at the village level, than the violence of the Khmer Rouge. At the end of its mission, the United Nations Transitional Authority in Cambodia (UNTAC) concluded that the country's history of repressive practices and the exercise of arbitrary authority persisted, and that Cambodia still had extremely weak institutions of law and order.[2] Lawlessness around the country continued to threaten progress in the advancement of human rights. There was an urgent need to rebuild (or build) those key institutions and structures vital for future human rights protection, including a functioning judiciary, an effective bureaucracy, and a professional police force.[3] While there have been some improvements in the criminal justice system since UNTAC's withdrawal, many of the appalling conditions still remain today. Cambodian society continues to need an independent judiciary, a politically neutral administration, a trained police force and army, a free press, viable state institutions capable of providing basic social services, a broadly educated professional class, and indigenous human rights organizations and other NGOs able and willing to promote and defend popular interests.[4]

In essence, the broad aim has to be to "civilianize" power in the community. This means transferring decisionmaking from the military to civilian public-sector units of administration. In questions concerning justice, summary military measures (which may be suitable in times of war) need to be replaced with independent judicial adjudication by civilian courts as peace settles throughout the country. Since UNTAC's time, the Phnom Penh government has asserted that its commitment to good governance and the establishment of the rule of law is central to the evolution of both Cambodia's democracy and its liberal market economy. The government has acknowledged that there must be changing patterns of societal behavior (particularly in combating corruption), and transformation of Cambodian society into one that respects fundamental ethical standards deriving from (1) the creation of a body of law, an impartial judicial and enforcement process, and a transparent and accountable public service; and (2) a respect for human rights, social justice, fairness, the immutable sanctity of contracts, and personal honesty and integrity.[5]

The Cambodian government has stated that some aspects of these principles are not always respected either in society as a whole or in the official bureaucracy, in the civil service and army; and it recognizes that Cambodian law and its enforcement are deficient in several respects. Furthermore, it has acknowledged the need for an effective and neutral government as a prerequisite for the success of its national program of rehabilitation and development. The government says that it is fully conscious of the fact that "the current inadequacies and gaps in the operating legal system could delay the rehabilitation of the country."[6] The ultimate objective of its initiatives, it has stated, is to lay the foundations for good governance and the rule of law. The "rule of law" as claimed to be understood by the Cambodian government presupposes that executive powers and instruments of administration are circumscribed by the scope of legislated provisions. As such, the government appreciates that the restoration of the rule of law is an ambitious goal.

To this end, Phnom Penh has set out its proposals for the reform of state institutions.[7] Officials recognized that the situation, without urgently needed changes, could foster nontransparency, insecurity, and the lack of legal rights and guarantees. Complementing the necessary legal framework, the Cambodian government is seeking to implement mechanisms for adequate legal control. The legal infrastructure for business and investment is considered to be conspicuously deficient. In addition to major gaps in commercial laws, significant lacunae plague such areas as dispute resolution and law enforcement generally. Naturally enough, lack of accountability has an adverse and deterrent effect on would-be entrepreneurs and potential investors. The government is endeavoring to create a proper legislative, institutional, and judicial framework, and it is in the process of reforming its civil service to reflect internationally accepted standards and the need for effective organs of state. It also intends to ensure that its army operates only under the effective authority and control of the government.[8]

The Cambodian government's broad strategy for introducing good governance and the rule of law thus centers on: (1) establishing the proper legislative, institutional, and judicial framework; (2) combating corruption; and (3) changing societal behavior gradually over the long term. Yet a number of fundamental observations can be made about the state of the law in Cambodia. Generally, there is a paucity of adequate legislative provisions necessary for the functioning of a modern state. In some areas, the Cambodian government has acknowledged that "although a body of law exists, it is imprecise."[9] Cambodia's existing legal and regulatory framework in general, and its capacity to enforce existing laws and regulations in particular, are exceedingly weak.[10] These conditions are a direct result of past destruction of the prevailing legal system and underlying institutions. Any legal culture has been completely absent in Cambodia in recent history.

Nevertheless, with a national assembly functioning under the new constitution since UNTAC, significant work has been undertaken to fill the legal vacuum in the administration of Cambodia. Regrettably, this has fallen far short of what is required for the most basic of laws. Although fundamental human rights are enshrined in the constitution, they become empty words unless they are scrupulously observed by the government and enforceable by the suit of the citizen before the courts. To put a body of available law and a functioning judiciary into effect is of vital importance if the rights referred to in the constitution are to have any meaning for Cambodians. The absence of a rule of law is still the greatest impediment to the protection of human rights in the country. The basic ingredient needed to reestablish legal order—now, just as it was during UNTAC—is a proper, functioning criminal justice system. The Cambodian experience is an invaluable example of a UN peace mission more flawed than successful. A violent, de facto coup by co-Prime Minister Hun Sen in July 1997 effectively erased a $2–3 billion election.[11] The lesson is that without justice there can be no prospect of a lasting peace.[12]

Requirements for Law and Order

Whether it was in Cambodia, Somalia, or Haiti, in Rwandan or Thai refugee camps, or in UN-controlled areas of the former Yugoslavia, general lawlessness not only hampered or denied progress toward peace but also in the interim seriously thwarted the UN's own operations. Humanitarian relief (such as the provision of food and medical services) has on many occasions proved impossible to deliver in the face of well-armed banditry. Early restoration of the rule of law will always make for safer peace-maintenance. If achieved, it will also reduce the level of military security that is required, which in turn will lead to much cheaper missions. The utility of some degree of law and order in the early phases of peace-maintenance is self-evident.

Experience to date has shown that the most serious human rights abuse during later periods of deployment tends to be the summary murder of political opponents by the local military and police, who at the same time enjoy complete immunity from the due process of any law. In UN operational theaters, arbitrary executions are performed unchecked, without hindrance or redress. All other human rights breaches usually pale in significance to this horrible reality. The core feature of any rule of law is provision for a functioning criminal justice system. Hence, the establishment of a judiciary is a priority in human rights observance and peace-maintenance. Creating mechanisms for the facilitation of justice through domestic legal systems is fundamentally a matter for UN transitional authorities.

Although UN missions have fielded considerable numbers of military contingents and some civilian police and human rights lawyers, scant attention has been paid to selection and training for their role in the reestablishment of justice. Apart from vague notions about their instructions to monitor law and order, little care has been taken in long-range strategic planning or provision of adequate resources for the task.

Many UN officials lament their previous failures to deliver justice and feel condemned to repeat the mistakes of the past in future postings. The role of UN lawyers and police has been characterized by ambiguity of authority and by frustration that they cannot use professional skills from long careers. These serving and former UN operatives have a wealth of experience acquired in recent years, which is in danger of being dissipated unless it is gathered and documented now. The distillation of this material can help create a set of practical tools for future peace-maintenance. Doing so involves the development of preparatory procedures and concept documents for incorporation in UN mandates and peace agreements, together with field manuals, resources, and materials for missions reestablishing the rule of law.

To this end, Australia has proposed the formulation of "justice packages" for UN peace missions. In his "blue book," Australian foreign affairs minister Sen. Gareth Evans summed up the lessons learned:

> The building of a functioning criminal justice system is a particularly crucial priority if the gains of a peace keeping operation are to be consolidated and a relapse into conflict avoided. We support the idea, advanced by lawyers in Cambodia troubled by their inability to effectively implement UNTAC's human rights mandate, that UN 'justice packages' be part of any peace keeping and post-conflict peace building exercises in countries where the rule of law, and the institutions needed to support it, have manifestly broken down. Elements of such a package would include provision, as appropriate, of a body of criminal law and procedures, drawing on universal principles; civil police, with training as well as law enforcement responsibilities; a panel of judges, prosecutors and defenders able to work with available local professionals during the transitional period, again with an obligation to train their local successors; and adequate correctional facilities, and personnel to staff them while developing local replacements. Basic as all these requirements may be, no viable government or social order can be built without them, and there will be situations where only the authority of the UN is capable of delivering them.[13]

UN planners and implementors find themselves constantly in a state of policy and administrative paralysis as they invariably debate the moral dilemmas afresh. A practical manual drawing on the experiences of recent operations should be prepared to guide the evolution of peace-maintenance. And a set of specific protocols ought to be developed for each particular crisis as it arises. Much to this discussion appears trite and so elementary that it goes without saying. Regrettably, however, experience has shown that basic principles are startling novelties to UN mission heads.

Such documents could also be published for the parties to a conflict, so that all the ramifications of the requirements of justice under a transitional authority are appreciated. The handing over of violators, access to their records, and respect for and enforcement of judicial decisions within the peace-maintenance framework require a full understanding by the protagonists; this will prevent them from dodging the difficult decisions of cooperating with the UN justice system when it comes to dealing with offenders in their own ranks.

The details of a particular justice package will vary from situation to situation. Each package has to be individually designed to meet the criminal justice needs of a particular people, such as to win their confidence—by making a difference in their lives, according to Clement Adibe. A justice package incorporates the generic nuts and bolts of law and order restoration, as well as local social and cultural dynamics for its acceptance by the population. Ultimately, success is determined by public confidence in the UN-initiated system to deliver justice, most important at the local level but also at the international level. The individuals directly concerned must be prepared to support it. As the experiences of Cambodia, Somalia, Haiti, and the former Yugoslavia demonstrate, there may be considerable diversity in how the people of these places see justice to be administered; many common elements inevitably flow, however, from the collapse of the nation-state into anarchy.

The aim of a justice package is to create a social compact, whereby the people of the country recently in conflict voluntarily agree to a system of law and order. A successful justice package brings about their cooperation. Ensuring community participation is essential if the UN does not want to find itself compelled to adopt military measures to enforce the law. Criminal justice systems initiated and designed by the UN must therefore be culturally sensitive and acceptable to the population concerned, and must at the same time accord with basic UN standards.

Furthermore, an independent judiciary is essential not only for a functioning criminal justice system and the enforcement of human rights but also as a financial imperative. Postconflict economic reconstruction will be hampered and foreign investment will not enter a country unless business has the assurance of a court system that will operate as an impartial commercial arbitrator between outside companies, commercial entities in the country, and the government of that country. Internal economic growth also demands the establishment of an independent and fair umpire for the expeditious resolution of commercial disputation. As Antonio Donini illustrates in the next chapter, repression is not just wrong, it is also bad for business.[14]

Dimensions of Justice Packages

The core objectives of a justice package are to: create a functioning criminal justice system; establish an independent, impartial and competent judiciary; appoint public prosecutors and defenders; train a responsible, respected police force with a strong sense of public service; build humane detention centers; and cónduct legal education. Justice packages are particularly applicable in the postconflict stage of peace-maintenance. They are designed to reestablish the operation of the rule of law in a country where it has collapsed or been so substantially eroded as not to function to meet the needs of the community.

For a justice package to succeed, the people must have confidence in the criminal justice system. This will require belief in the impartiality and professionalism of police to apprehend accused offenders. It requires public trust in an independent, fair, and competent judiciary. And it requires the commitment of the local authorities, not only to enforce and observe the decisions of the judiciary but also to be prepared to submit themselves to its judgment. Military, police, and public officials accused of crimes must be surrendered to the will of the criminal justice system. This means that acquittals and convictions need to be accepted and prison sentences enforced. Also, judges themselves must have security or tenure and physical protection. The following matters should be agreed on prior to the deployment of a peace-maintenance operation.

A UN criminal law and procedure. A legal basis has to be provided for the creation of the criminal justice system during the immediate and transitionary phase. A long-established and respected body of law may be resurrected for this purpose. In Somalia, the former Italian Penal Code was utilized. In Cambodia, the Vietnamese-drawn criminal law and procedure articulated in great detail counterrevolutionary crimes, but it was woefully unworkable to achieve the UN's fundamental objectives. Accordingly, UNTAC drafted and caused to be enacted its own law; it too fell short of basic UN standards. For example, the absence of consent was not included as an element of the offense of rape, and no legal defenses were set out. The point is, if the UN is to introduce its own laws and conduct its own prosecutions, then the laws and procedures must comply with the UN's own standards.

Where no law exists, a UN "off-the-shelf" criminal law and procedure is essential in any peace-maintenance arsenal.[15] In the first instance, such a law is necessary to deal with the most serious of violent criminal offenses—such as murder, abduction, arson, and assault. As the semblances of the rule of law are restored, more sophisticated prohibitions against corruption and discrimination can be introduced. Wherever they exist, UN codifications, conventions, and precedents will be drawn on for the proposed criminal law and procedure, such as: the 1948 Universal Declaration of Human Rights; the 1966 International Covenant on Civil and Political Rights; the Basic Principles on the Independence of the Judiciary;[16] the Code of Conduct for Law Enforcement Officials;[17] the International Law Commission's Draft Statute for an International Criminal Court;[18] and the Guidelines on the Role of Prosecutors.[19] The basic law and procedure could be based upon the Draft Code of Crimes Against the Peace and Security of Mankind[20] and would need to comply with existing UN standards for the administration of justice. The experience of the International Tribunal for the Former Yugoslavia based at the Hague is leading the way in this area and still very much in the learning phase. The definition of offenses, together with defenses, procedures, and rules of evidence, may generally evolve from this country-specific Security Council initiative.

Panel of distinguished international jurists. A panel of distinguished international jurists, either retired or serving judges, should be available on call ready to preside or provide on-the-job training for locals. The ad hoc nature of the Yugoslav tribunal is a precedent for this exercise.[21] A hearing before UN judges will often constitute the only forum for the conduct of some trials, when either the local courts will not act or the accused, victims, and witnesses are from different factions than the trial court. Another variation is to appoint a panel of trial judges and/or jurors from across the factions, with a distinguished international jurist in the chair. Where courts are created, it will also be necessary to create appeal courts.

UN special prosecutions. In the early stages of a peace-maintenance mission, no independent judiciary or effective police force may exist. The UN will be required to assume the tasks of arrest, prosecution, and trial of serious offenders, when the local officials will not act or are in fact the criminal perpetrators. This will be essential where major human rights breaches are being committed by the leadership of the existing factions, which threaten the neutral political environment and imperil free and fair elections. The special prosecutor must be independent from the UN mission hierarchy,[22] as was provided for the Yugoslav tribunal prosecutors. A UN prosecution policy should be established to guide the prosecution criteria and, especially, clarify how to decide when not to try a case. Political considerations and expediency cannot play a part in this consideration. The extraordinarily large numbers of offenders in a Rwanda-type situation may require selectivity of prosecution, or the impossibility of prosecution, as in Somalia, may require resort to the inquiry mode with general findings, as set out below.

Specialized resources. Essential to any UN special prosecution are forensic science facilities, such as autopsies pathology. The UN has developed a model autopsy protocol, as well as a postmortem torture detection procedure.[23] Most missions simply have not had the resources to perform basic post mortems or ballistic work. These produce necessary forms of prosecutory evidence. Cross-cultural and religious views may require some variation of these procedures. Also, an underestimated resource-consuming need in UN missions is a proper witness protection program, to ensure the safety of informants and their families in order to bring about successful prosecutions. This may require permanent relocation of victims and witnesses. In the apprehension of criminals, the use of rewards and indemnities are useful tools and should be considered. Again, definitive UN policies and criteria should be spelled out.

Commissions of inquiry. In addition to judges ready to preside over trials, others should be prepared to sit as commissions of inquiry, like the truth commissions in El Salvador and South Africa. Such inquiries, given lesser standards of proof, may be used to stop human rights violators by either publishing their abuses as a deterrent or administratively disqualifying them from existing office or election to office. A prime purpose of these inquiries is to air public concern, bring transgressors to account, and embarrass wrongdoers without the need for trials. Further, holding inquiries can be instrumental in initiating local reforms. The UN has to settle the terms of reference, powers, and procedures for such inquiries.

Survey and assessment of existing justice assets. An assessment of the existing justice assets should be made of the country that is likely to require peace-maintenance, since these will be built on, developed, and improved. The survey needs to determine the state of the domestic law, the cost of capital works for jails and courtrooms, and the cost of training for judges, lawyers, and police. Long-range forward survey work and scenario planning should precede any peace-maintenance mission. Some countries, as was the case with Cambodia before the Paris agreements, can be seen as likely candidates for UN intervention well in advance of the final formulation of a peace accord. Early exchange programs for lawyers and police would assist them in getting to know the local personnel, so as to ease the facilitation of the justice package.

Selection of acceptable local personnel. Since the restoration of peace is about the "civilianization" of power, one way to transfer administrative decisionmaking is to harness the leadership assets of the generals by turning them into heads of civilian units of public administration. To reempower the citizenry, it may be necessary to civilianize the military. Bridges have to be built between career paths to enable genuine leadership skills to be reutilized. Ultimately, acceptance of the rule of law is about establishing public confidence in the courts. A social compact has evolved when the populace agree to resolve their disputes through words rather than bullets. In this sense, there will be many existing personnel who will be entirely unacceptable because of their involvement in war crimes, human rights abuses, and oppression.[24]

Judicial training. Article 14(1) of the International Covenant on Civil and Political Rights provides that everyone shall be entitled to a fair and public hearing by a competent and impartial tribunal established by law. Article 10 of the UN Basic Principles on the Independence of the Judiciary provides that persons selected for judicial office shall be individuals of integrity and ability with appropriate training or qualifications in law. To fulfill these provisions, a program for judicial training needs to be devised as part of any justice package.

In Phnom Penh, the UN Special Representative for Human Rights in Cambodia, Justice Michael Kirby, urged the introduction of a system of judicial mentors and advisors.[25] The Cambodia office of the UN Centre for Human Rights consequently proposed a judicial mentoring project.[26] With a view to improving the judicial system, the project would be designed to provide to Cambodian judges on-site training and assistance in the implementation of human rights and criminal law. The mentors would be experienced international lawyers and retired judges, who would be assigned to provincial courts and coordinated in the capital. The proposed program recognizes: the need to increase the technical capacity of the courts to act independently, in conformity with Cambodian law and international human rights standards; the need for technical assistance in the organization of the courts and their conduct of procedure; the need for advisory support in resolving legal issues without interfering in the decisionmaking process; the need to increase coordination between courts and law enforcement agencies; the need to assist in the implementation of legislation; and the need to lay the groundwork for an ongoing and long-term overhaul of the judicial system.[27]

The overall objectives of such projects would be to: (1) assist Cambodian courts in implementing legislation in conformity with international human rights standards; (2) assist in improving coordination between courts, prison officials, the police, the military, and provincial administration; (3) assist the judges in the day-to-day functioning of courts relating to their organization, procedure, and law; and (4) prepare an assessment for a long-term overhaul of the judicial system, and identify the policy and legal changes necessary to achieve such an overhaul.

Police training. A vital task for UN police will be the training of a local responsible constabulary in community policing. In Cambodia, the deficiencies of CIVPOL began with the selection of personnel by the UN. Many of the CIVPOL chosen were not police at all. What Cambodia required was, first, good community police and, second, trained investigators who understood the apprehension of offenders, the collection of evidence, and the preparation of prosecutions. A form of UN accreditation should ensure that those selected are police trained to the requisite standard for a peace-maintenance mission. This includes a special emphasis on community policing, where the police have experience in mediation for the resolution of disputes.[28]

The independence of CIVPOL officers. Although the police may have the outward semblance of a military force, the command structure is, in an operational sense, the reverse. Like the special prosecutor, the police require independence from the UN hierarchy. A constable is expected to exercise individually his or her arrest and prosecuting discretion. In the discharge of duties, when intervening in a dispute between offender and victim, a constable is not subject to the direction of an immediate superior. In the decision to arrest or not to arrest, to prosecute or not to prosecute, a constable is answerable only to the court. As the General Assembly observed when it adopted the UN's Code of Conduct for Law Enforcement Officials, "there are additional important principles and prerequisites for the humane performance of law enforcement functions, namely . . . [t]hat, like all agencies of the criminal justice system, every law enforcement agency should be representative of and responsive and accountable to the community as a whole." This accountability is to an independent judiciary, not up the chain of command. Police are trained to use minimum force in a conflict, whereas the military are trained to use maximum force. Justice systems are answerable to the people through courts, not through executive government. For these reasons, CIVPOL should not be integrated within a military component. Although there should be closer coordination of and clearer definitions for CIVPOL and better tools to do the job, CIVPOL should and must remain independent from the military.

Training of prosecutors and defenders. Local prosecutors and defense counsel will require training. A prosecutor has a heavy duty to ensure that an accused person receives a fair trial. The UN and its trained personnel must be model litigants. The performance of a prosecutor's professional duties and obligations, in determining whether a prosecution is to be commenced, is independent of political considerations or directions from legislative and executive functionaries: "in the final analysis the prosecutor is not a servant of government or individuals—he or she is a servant of justice."[29] The prosecutor is answerable to the courts for any misconduct and not to an administrative hierarchy.[30] As lawyers, prosecutors have not only a professional obligation but also an ethical duty to see that the law is respected and upheld "to the best of [their] capability, [and to] prevent and rigorously oppose any violation."[31]

Detention centers. Construction will have to be undertaken of jails and detention centers that are environmentally humane for inmates and consistent with the UN Standard Minimum Rules for the Treatment of Prisoners.[32] Ironically, the UN had to build jails in Cambodia, after all of its unhappy history, to prevent arbitrary executions. At the same time as detention facilities are built, measures must also be incorporated in any justice package to reduce prison populations where appropriate. The essential requirements include prison custody diversion programs, bail procedures, early release, and alternatives to imprisonment. A dilemma arises from the construction of detention centers where the minimum standards are applied: prisoners, who are the outcasts of society, may be better housed and fed than nearby villagers. This disparity can breed resentment of the UN, or worse still, create incentives to be taken into custody.

Alternatives to imprisonment. The mediation, dispute resolution, and reconciliation roles of CIVPOL can be alternatives to arrest, detention, and prosecution. Without idealizing forms of informal dispute resolution[33] (as there is no assessment of their effectiveness in achieving genuine reconciliation and consistency with international human rights standards), they do, however, offer ways to settle many quasi-criminal and criminal complaints by one person against another. This can be done without the intervention of the state, except to the extent necessary, when directed or mediated by the police or a village chief. So too, the UN must develop diversionary programs as part of any penalties that a court may impose.

Physical security for justice personnel. Physical security for judges, prosecutors, defenders, police, and jailers may be called for, as well as witness protection. During UNTAC, the local courts refused to hear UN prosecutions for fear of retribution. The Phnom Penh government had instructed the judges not to consider UN cases. They obeyed that order in usurpation of their required independence because of fear of reprisals to their families and for their own personal safety. After the UN's departure, the failure of the courts' judicial independence was entirely subsumed in a more daunting reality of the physical vulnerability of officials who exercised their duties. Those courts that have been brave enough to uphold respect for the rule of law have encountered serious problems in enforcing their decisions against military officials. In many cases, judges and court personnel have been subject to threats, attacks, and attempted murder.[34]

This violence has been thoroughly documented by others, but in making any assessment of the feasibility and risk of proposals for assistance to the judiciary, it is instructive to reflect upon illustrative transgressions. In the first year following UNTAC, threats to and the thwarting of judges, particularly from military and political authorities, were serious challenges to the rule of law and had increased manifold. This resulted in lawlessness, arbitrary violence, and the denial of basic human rights.[35] In Sihanoukville, on 13 May 1994, heavily armed military elements attacked the chief judge and the prosecutor and disrupted court proceedings. A military officer, whose parents had been found guilty of a trademark offense and who had been sentenced but not yet committed to prison, invaded the court building in the company of other armed military personnel. The judge and prosecutor were forced to flee for their lives. The response by the authorities was woefully inadequate. The military personnel were not prosecuted and the parents remained unpunished. In Battambang, on 29 March 1994, soldiers reportedly from the Fourth Military Region stormed the town prison, threatening the lives of guards and other inmates, to release a prisoner who had been convicted and incarcerated for smuggling Khmer antiquities from Cambodia into Thailand. Armed military elements disrupted scheduled trials on 7 July 1994 at the Phnom Penh municipal court, and on 15 July 1994 at Kandal court. There was an arbitrary killing of a civilian by military elements at Stung Treng and nonprosecution of the case.[36] The special representative for human rights has received complaints from the judiciary concerning these abuses of authority and the difficulty, in practice, of bringing those responsible before the courts for punishment.[37]

Anticorruption measures. A much neglected area of law enforcement that vexes the provision and distribution of resources, often of considerable sums much needed by the people, is the adoption of anticorruption measures. This involves ethics training, financial and conflict of interest disclosure, development of codes of conduct, and sophisticated fraud and audit detection mechanisms for public officials.

Adequate legal resources. Many countries lack basic legal materials and texts. In Cambodia, the provision of even outdated and discarded text books proved invaluable to local jurists and law enforcement officials seeking solutions to domestic problems from the models and precedents of other jurisdictions. The scale of inadequate resources extends from the complete absence of any legal texts in some provincial courts, to less than subsistence salaries paid by the state to judges, right down to a shortage of clerical materials necessary for a functioning court, such as filing cabinets, desks, pens, and paper. Many courts do not have copies of the existing laws that they are required to interpret and enforce. The courts need these basic provisions, as well as photocopiers and funds for clerical and investigative staff.

Many courts are in a run-down state, and repairs at a small cost would greatly enhance their community prestige and the working conditions of judges. The court of appeal in Phnom Penh was restored with international assistance for a modest sum. The provincial court at Battambang benefited from inexpensive repairs and painting.[38] If a prison reconstruction project were to be considered, any cost surveys of provincial prisons should also include assessing the cost estimates of court repairs. The local court house should not only be a focal point for the administration of justice but also a visible architectural symbol of the reestablishment of the rule of law.

The courts are assisted by clerks whose standard of education is very basic. Most have grown up under a communist system and have little understanding about the proper role of courts in democratic society. Their files are a mess. In most court houses, documents litter the floors. The clerks have no typewriters or filing facilities. When supplying material to defense lawyers they usually part with the originals. Assistance by an international lawyer to upgrade the records of the court in Battambang proved to be beneficial.[39] The clerks were enthusiastic about implementing an efficient filing system, but there are risks that such gains may be short-lived if not followed up. Funds for generators and Khmer script wordprocessors are much needed. Modest assistance to the conditions of the clerks would significantly improve the functioning of the courts.

Financial Implications of Law and Order

In the case of Cambodia—followed throughout this chapter—despite the existence of new constitutionally guaranteed rights and a criminal law procedure, the courts are too weak to enforce the law and prevent the arbitrary abuse of authority. The Cambodian Justice Department budget is one of the weakest and poorest of all government departments, receiving some 0.2 percent of the overall public service budget.[40] From this, the wages of the police, prison officers, prosecutors, and judges must be met, as must capital requirements of equipment, the repair of buildings and food for prisoners. This meager fiscal allocation graphically illustrates the low priority of developing the rule of law. If there is to be a commitment to institution building through the reestablishment of law and order, then there must be a diversion of funds to departments of justice, which are required to administer not only courts but the police and prisons as well. Ultimately, an appropriate measure of budgetary independence must be provided for the judiciary if it is to be genuinely a separate organ of the state performing the functions required by a constitution. Accordingly, a key part of a UN justice package is to put in place proper budgetary measures and financial standards for justice.

Postoperational procedures for auditing the performance of local staff, following the transfer of functions to them from UN personnel, would also be a feature of the justice package. The use of a special rapporteur is a small part of such a program. Continued funding after the peace-maintenance exercise may be used to ensure the observance of judicial decisions made by the international authority during the transitional period. Schemes have to be devised for the enforcement of judicial decisions in the wake of withdrawal. An international justice fund to which interested nations, various national legal professions, and corporate entities contribute could be used to pay for the justice package and ongoing assistance. Secure salaries are needed for the judges, prosecutors, defenders, police, and jailers. In Third World countries, this is comparatively inexpensive. The average annual income for a Cambodian during UNTAC was the equivalent of U.S.

$150. The cost of an entire justice system under these circumstances is inexpensive and attainable. It is certainly cheaper than the extremely high cost of military hardware. ⊕

Notes

Mark Plunkett is a practicing barrister-at-law in Brisbane, Australia, and was formerly the special prosecutor in the United Nations Transitional Authority in Cambodia (UNTAC). He has written extensively on the development of "justice packages" for peace operations.

1. See, for insance, Karen Kenny, *Towards Effective Training for Field Human Rights Tasks* (Dublin: International Human Rights Trust, 1996); Institute of Policy Studies (IPS) of Singapore and United Nations Institute for Training and Research (UNITAR), *The Role and Functions of Civilian Police in United Nations Peace-Keeping Operations: Debriefing and Lessons* (The Hague: Kluwer Law International, 1996).

2. UNTAC Doc., "Human Rights Component Final Report," Phnom Penh, September 1993, p. 2.

3. Ibid., p. 5.

4. United Nations Centre for Human Rights, "Programme of Advisory Services and Technical Assistance: The Judicial Mentor Programme," March 1995.

5. Kingdom of Cambodia, "Position Paper on Reinforcing the Rule of Law," Paris, March 1995.

6. Kingdom of Cambodia, "Implementing the National Programme to Rehabilitate and Develop Cambodia," February 1995, p. 14, and see generally pp. 14–24.

7. Ibid., pp. 14, 24.

8. Kingdom of Cambodia, "Position Paper on Reinforcing the Rule of Law."

9. Kingdom of Cambodia, "Implementing the National Programme to Rehabilitate and Develop Cambodia," p. 14.

10. World Bank, "Cambodia Rehabilitation Program: Implementation Outlook; A World Bank Report for the ICORC Conference," February 1995, par. 3.4, p. 29.

11. Compare Keith B. Richburg and R. Jeffrey Smith, "What Went Wrong in Cambodia?" and Fred Hiatt, "A Dying Peace in Cambodia," *The Washington Post,* 28 July 1997, national weekly edition, pp. 14–15, p. 29, respectively. See also Nate Thayer, "In Cambodia, A Truce That Almost Was," *The Washington Post,* 25 August 1997, national weekly edition, pp. 15–16.

12. Human Rights Watch/Asia, *Cambodia at War* (New York: Human Rights Watch, 1995).

13. Gareth Evans, *Cooperating for Peace: The Global Agenda for the 1990s and Beyond* (St. Leonards, N.S.W.: Allen & Unwin, 1993), p. 56; see also p. 110.

14. K. English and A. Stapleton, *The Human Rights Handbook: A Practical Guide to Monitoring Human Rights* (Essex, England: Human Rights Centre, University of Essex, October 1995), p. 4.

15. Compare Amnesty International, "Peace-keeping and human rights," AI Doc. IOR 40/01/94 of January 1994, pp. 35–45.

16. Adopted by the Eighth United Nations Congress on the Prevention of Crime and Treatment of Offenders, 1990.

17. Adopted by the UN General Assembly in Resolution 34/169 of 17 December 1979. See also, Crime Prevention and Criminal Justice Branch, *United*

Nations Criminal Justice Standards for Peace-Keeping Police (Vienna: United Nations, February 1994).

18. Compare Andy Knight, "Legal Issues," in John Tessitore and Susan Woolfson, eds., *A Global Agenda: Issues Before the 51st General Assembly* (Lanham, Md.: Rowman and Littlefield Publishers, 1996), pp. 262–265 and 268–282.

19. Adopted by the Eighth United Nations Congress on the Prevention of Crime and the Treatment of Offenders, 1990.

20. Compare Timothy L. H. McCormack and Gerry J. Simpson, "The International Law Commission's Draft Code of Crimes against the Peace and Security of Mankind: An Appraisal of the Substantive Provisions," *Criminal Law Forum* 5, no. 1 (1994): 1–55; Knight, "Legal Issues," pp. 265–268.

21. Compare Maj. Michael Kelly, *Peace Operations: Tackling the Military Legal and Policy Challenges* (Canberra: Australian Government Publishing Service, 1997), chap. 6.

22. Human Rights Watch, *The Lost Agenda: Human Rights and U.N. Field Operations* (New York: Human Rights Watch, 1993), pp. 62–63.

23. See UN Centre for Social Development and Humanitarian Affairs, *Manual on the Effective Prevention and Investigation of Extra-Legal, Arbitrary and Summary Executions* (New York: United Nations, 1991).

24. Compare The Washington Office on Latin America, *Demilitarizing Public Order: The International Community, Police Reform and Human Rights in Central America and Haiti* (Washington, D.C.: The Washington Office on Latin America, November 1995).

25. United Nations Commission on Human Rights, "Situation of Human Rights in Cambodia: Report of the Special Representative of the Secretary-General for Human Rights in Cambodia, Mr. Michael Kirby," UN Doc. E/CN.4/1995/87/ Add. 1 of 13 February 1995, par. 23, p. 10.

26. United Nations Centre for Human Rights, "Judicial Mentor Programme," June 1995.

27. Ibid., par. 2.

28. Compare Martin R. Ganzglass, "The Restoration of the Somali Justice System," in Walter Clarke and Jeffrey Herbst, eds., *Learning From Somalia: The Lessons of Armed Humanitarian Intervention* (Boulder: Westview, 1997), pp. 20–41.

29. Commonwealth Director of Public Prosecutions, *The Prosecution Policy of the Commonwealth* (Canberra: Australian Government Publishing Service, 1992), par. 6.1, p. 24.

30. See the Guidelines on the Role of Prosecutors, which provides: in Article 3 that "Prosecutors, as essential agents of the administration of justice, shall at all times maintain the honour and dignity of their professions"; in Article 4 that "States should ensure that prosecutors are able to perform their professional functions without intimidation, hindrance, harassment, improper interference or unjustified exposure to civil, penal or other liability"; and in Article 13 that "In the performance of their duties, prosecutors shall: (a) Carry out their functions impartially and avoid all political, social, religious, racial, cultural, sexual or any other kind of discrimination; (b) Protect the public interest, act with objectivity, take proper account of the position of the suspect and the victim, pay attention to all relevant circumstances, irrespective of whether they are to the advantage or disadvantage of the suspect."

31. This is most aptly enshrined in Article 8 of the Code of Conduct for Law Enforcement Officials.

32. Adopted by the Economic and Social Council in Resolution 663 (XXIV) of 31 July 1957.

33. Lindsay E. Harris, *Women and the Cambodian Legal System: A Woman's Legal Needs and Assessments* (Phnom Penh: Asia Foundation, February 1994), p. 63.

34. United Nations Centre for Human Rights, "The Judicial Mentor Programme," March 1995.

35. Report of the Secretary-General, "Situation of Human Rights in Cambodia: Recommendations of the Special Representative for Human Rights in Cambodia and the Role of the United Nations Centre for Human Rights in Assisting the Government and People of Cambodia in the Promotion and Protection of Human Rights," UN Doc. A/49/635 of 3 November 1994, par. 51, p. 19.

36. Ibid., par. 77–82, p. 27.

37. United Nations, "Report of the Special Representative," 13 February 1995, par. 24, p. 11.

38. Asia Foundation, *The Battambang Law Court Project—Final Report*, June 1994.

39. Ibid.

40. Australian International Development Assistance Bureau figure, cited in Ibid., par. 2.1.

5

Asserting Humanitarianism
in Peace-Maintenance

———————— ⊕ ————————

Antonio Donini

This chapter is about the rise and fall of humanitarianism as a paradigm in international relations. It will look at humanitarianism as an imperative, as a "mobilizing myth," and as a contemporary form of containment. It will attempt to show how these three dimensions have altered our conceptualization of North-South relations. It will look at the evolution of humanitarian practice in the post–Cold War years, attempt to define the function of humanitarian assistance in the contexts of globalization of the economy and of the failure of development models, and propose avenues of further reflection for policymakers, practitioners, and scholars. It will look at the role of humanitarian assistance in peace operations and discuss the advantages and disadvantages of mixing politics and relief, particularly in the delicate peace consolidation phase. Finally, it will argue that short-term strategies in countries in crisis are recipes for failure, and that the new paradigm waiting to emerge, like peace-maintenance, must be based on a strategic vision integrating politics, relief, and development for the long haul.

The Geopolitics of Mercy

The statistical world war of the 1990s, described at the beginning of this book, has been matched by an unprecedented increase in the need for humanitarian assistance. With some 120 "active" wars, and more starting each year than ending, never since 1945 has conflict-related human suffering reached such levels: more than forty million refugees and internally displaced persons require help. Tens of millions more do not show up in the figures of the international community: those who are affected by war in their communities with no possibility of escape; those who are reduced to abject poverty because of the breakdown of governance and international safety nets; and those who did not make it, the direct and indirect casualties of organized violence.

While respect for humanitarian norms, and in particular for the fundamental right of victims to receive assistance, has been in recent years tenuous at best, 1994—the year of genocide in Rwanda—will be remembered as a watershed in the annals of brutality. Rwanda has deeply affected the humanitarian community. It has challenged some of the very concepts of humanitarianism: that is, the moral principles and operational tenets that govern, or should govern, humanitarian action.[1] The shadow of genocide is likely to have an important impact on how humanitarians will look upon future crises and, perhaps, even on the shape of the institutions of the international community. The deliberate targeting of relief workers by warring factions and the increasing instances of open manipulation of humanitarian assistance for military or political gain are likely to have a similar effect. For many, a system that results in an equanimous impartiality between the victims and the executioners is in dire need of reform. Indeed, a number of reform proposals have been put on the table.[2]

The end of bipolarity and the increase in the number of crises initially fueled a parallel, and for a while exponential, growth in UN peace operations. One of the paradoxical consequences of the end of the Cold War was the sudden appearance of the military in the humanitarian arena, a front where they were seldom seen in the past. Working with or close to the military has not always been easy. Cultural and operational differences have been the source of friction on both sides. This has had an impact on the activities of UN humanitarian organizations, both at the institutional and conceptual levels, and for practical coordination on the ground. Despite efforts to reconcile peacekeeping goals with the imperatives of humanitarian assistance, concern is still widespread among humanitarian agencies about the appropriateness, and the costs, of mixing soldiers and relief. In late 1996, such concern turned to outright frustration at the inability of the international community to deploy its military might even in the face of massive human suffering and human rights violations in Burundi and Eastern Zaire.

Thus the context in which humanitarian assistance is provided is rapidly changing, becoming more brutal, more volatile, more dangerous. War itself is an altogether different reality.[3] It used to be a matter for states, or at least for groups aspiring to statehood and legitimacy. Roles are now increasingly blurred: it is often difficult to distinguish the military from the civilian, the oppressed from the oppressor, and even the police force from the fire brigade and the ambulance corps. The red cross and the blue flag, once protecting symbols, have now become fair game. Armed bandits and other "war-making entities" are not the best of interlocutors with whom to discuss humanitarian norms and freedom of access to victims. From Jaffna to Jalalabad and from Banja Luka to Butare, it is the civilians who are paying the heaviest price of contemporary warfare. They are pawns, hostages, and objects of conflict, if not the deliberate targets of violence. Looting is the corollary to warlordism, just as violence against civilians is the corollary to the breakdown of societies.

The current wave of internal wars is but one of the parameters that define the new environment in which humanitarian actors are compelled to intervene. In many ways, it is intervention itself that should be seen as the new defining element in the postbipolar world, rather than conflict, which of course existed throughout the previous decades, whether in the form of wars by proxy or in resistance to superpower hegemony. In recent years, there has been a kind of double lifting of inhibitions that had been largely suppressed by the rules of the Cold War game: the inhibition to wage war and the inhibition to intervene.

The humanitarians have become orphans of the Cold War. The changed context, the frequent absence of visible or understandable ideological stakes with which to identify, but perhaps more important, the lifting of the shackles that constrained diplomacy during the superpower rivalry, have made intervention of the humanitarian variety—that is, without taking sides (or, more precisely, taking the side of the victims)—easier to advocate and more palatable for the international community (and for the purse holders in donor countries). It has also facilitated intervention of the military variety—with knights in blue armor—in support of humanitarian objectives. For better or for worse, humanitarian assistance has become an essential ingredient in international relations.

While war and intervention may well be the most visible *innovations*, other architectural changes have accompanied the demise of the old order and the turbulent search for a new one. The environment in which structural breakdown and "emergencies" occur, and the atmosphere of North-South relations, has been radically changed.

To begin with, the international community, in its response to crises, has lifted a number of restrictions concerning sovereignty. In a world dominated by superpowers, respect for sovereignty was at best relative. But it is now clear that, whether or not it ever was, sovereignty is no longer sacrosanct. The members of the international community as a whole have been loathe to codify criteria for intervention, but in practice a number of interventions have taken place, which would have been unthinkable only a decade ago. For a brief moment, the illusion of a "new world order" led Northern leaders to believe that the forces unleashed by the end of the Cold War could be "treated" through more or less coherent integrated approaches to problem solving. Hence the notion of "complex emergency" and the acknowledgement of the linkages between the political, the military, and the humanitarian. And hence the recent, perhaps fleeting, flirtation with multilateral military intervention, whether to counter acts of aggression or in support of humanitarian objectives, or both.

This militarization of North-South relations raises a number of questions. Could it be that under the alibi of humanitarian action, military intervention is simply the clumsy expression of new forms of hegemony? Militarization is a powerful mechanism to force recalcitrant actors to conform and acquiesce. Intervention is by no means consistent: why Angola and not Afghanistan, why Somalia and not Sudan, why Liberia and not Zaire? This is not to say that militarization of humanitarian crises is necessarily guided by ulterior motives. Sometimes Northern powers are shamed into intervening by the pressure of public opinion or by *mediapolitik*. More often than not, however, the eternal rules of *realpolitik* guide the humanitarian helping hand.

The point here is that the international community does not appear to have made up its mind on whether the use of troops in humanitarian situations should be something truly exceptional, justifiable as a stopgap measure in only extreme circumstances where cost is not a primary concern, or whether the military are destined to become a regular feature of the world's humanitarian regime. From a humanitarian point of view, the pertinence of military intervention is at best doubtful. In Liberia, Somalia, and the former Yugoslavia, the cynical (or perhaps realist) view is that intervention has prolonged the conflict and has often created obstacles to the provision of humanitarian assistance. In Afghanistan, by contrast, the fact that there was no intervention allowed a "humanitarian consensus" to be negotiated among all factions and, in turn, the meeting of the most urgent humanitarian needs. Food aid was seldom stolen or hijacked, in part because it was mostly distributed by private truckers who had a vested interest in getting to their destination in order to obtain further UN contracts—unlike in Somalia where it was delivered by militarized and highly visible UN convoys.

The risks inherent in the militarization of humanitarian assistance cannot be underestimated. The broad question, therefore, is this: Should the humanitarians be better equipped by the international community to do their job or should the military be trained to take on tasks other than war and security?[4]

As for the market, it is debatable if it has ever suffered from any inhibitions. Its limits were dictated by ideological containment and Cold War barriers rather than by any moral qualms. What is interesting to note here is the increasing extension of market mechanisms to areas hitherto protected: the privatization of North-South relations, and in particular of humanitarian assistance. For four and a half decades, "overseas development assistance" and its junior cousin "emergency aid" were well within the realm of states. The end of the Cold War emboldened Western capitals; the inherent dysfunctions of working through governments, and the lessening urgency to support unpalatable regimes for ideological reasons, have led to the application of laissez-faire precepts in the conduct of international affairs. The invocation of privatization and of civil society often function as a smokescreen for the imposition of "political conditionality." This is particularly visible in postconflict settings like Mozambique, where the provision of large-scale aid packages was made contingent on the privatization of significant segments of the state—ranging from the transport of food aid to the national demining entity—on grounds that such structures were inefficient or "corrupt."[5] The result has been an extraordinary explosion of private sector intervention in the Third World, nowhere more visible than in the provision of relief.

Perhaps the most significant innovation in recent years is the extent to which in weak Third World societies nongovernmental organizations (NGOs) have taken over state-type functions, in areas like health and education, as well as the bulk of the delivery of relief services in faltering or failed states. Even in countries like Kenya or Zambia, increasingly large segments of the state, hitherto supported by state-to-state aid are now being privatized in the sense that external assistance goes directly to the implementing NGO and bypasses the local government.

In operational terms, this has led to the emergence of a competitive contract culture in the international NGO community.[6] In structural and ideological terms, this means that "development" has ceased to function as a "mobilizing myth" for the South. The only remaining system is the market, and for the many it is the rewards of "trickle-down" that are mythical. In practical terms, this means that the NGO community in the West has benefited significantly from the fact that, with the end of superpower confrontation, the imperative of North-South, state-to-state support has all but disappeared. The U.S. government, for instance, has set a target of 40 percent of its overseas development assistance (ODA) to be distributed through NGOs.[7] Will this be equally beneficial for the victims of conflict, for local coping mechanisms in crisis-affected countries, and for longer-term self-reliance? The answer is less than certain.

A related trend, which is shaping the environment in which humanitarian actors operate, is the extent to which resources and attention are being diverted from development to relief. The exponential growth of disbursements for humanitarian assistance is unquestionable: from barely $845 million a year in 1989 to close to $7 billion in 1996.[8] With the collapse of the Soviet bloc, the number of claimants for development aid has dramatically increased. Donors, however, tend to focus on the short term. Funds are generally available to save lives in emergencies but seem to be more difficult to come by for recovery and the reconstruction of livelihoods. Moreover, the combination of privatization and diversion of development resources to relief is likely to mean more political conditionality rather than less. For the donor, the reorientation of budgetary priorities toward quick-fix emergency relief provides an easy way to flex geopolitical muscles when apportioning the residual development assistance funds. Here again, past inhibitions are gone.[9]

As for the UN, for a brief historical moment, both member states and the Secretariat felt liberated. After forty years, the heavy lid of the Cold

War was lifted and the organization's *langue de bois*—its "bureaucratese," a kind of Orwellian "newspeak"—gave way to more open forms of expression. The ideals of the founding fathers seemed to come to life. During the year that preceded and the two years that followed the 1992 publication of the secretary-general's *Agenda for Peace*, much seemed possible. Until then, the UN regimes for peacekeeping, human rights, and humanitarian and development activities had been kept in separate, if not watertight, compartments, and the Security Council—when it was not deadlocked by crossed vetoes—dealt with security and not humanitarian questions. Issues suddenly refused to remain in neat bureaucratic boxes. The new wave of emergencies became "complex," mixing the political, the military, and the humanitarian. The military peacekeeping-interventionist approach became the new gospel, the implication for the humanitarians being that they should comply and integrate. The enthusiasm for peace operations peaked in 1994, when a record number of eighty thousand blue helmets were deployed. Bosnia and Somalia have had a sobering effect: extreme caution is likely to be exercised henceforth. The times of UN peace-enforcement may have come and gone. Regional coalitions of the willing may only selectively pick up the slack.

It remains to be seen if the current spate of complex emergencies is destined to become a permanent operational reality for the international community, or if it is only a transitory phase in the post–Cold War movement of tectonic plates. It also remains to be seen whether the donor community will be able to continue to mobilize the domestic will and the resources for both quick-fix emergency assistance and for longer-term development programs in the Third World. While serious prevention initiatives are nowhere in sight, donor exhaustion looms ominous.

Given the multiplication of crises and the increasing number of claimants on limited resources, short-term emergency needs are taking precedence over long-term development programs. Both bilateral donors and multilateral organizations have had to "divert." Just to give one example: the World Food Programme (WFP) used to be primarily a development and food-for-work organization; now 80 percent of its food resources are devoted to emergency feeding programs. Donor governments face difficult choices about how best to utilize their "kitty" for international assistance and how to balance financial priorities between military (peacekeeping and humanitarian support), relief, and development activities.

In these circumstances, it was perhaps to be expected that political conditionality should emerge under the guise of donor fatigue, or more precisely "development fatigue." Political conditionality—that is, "human rights and privatization first, development assistance later"—is a practical way of deflecting attention from some of the more disturbing dimensions of North-South relations. Structural issues have all but disappeared from the debate.[10] The present emphasis on "managerial" concepts, such as sustainable development and global governance, which do not really address the nature of underdevelopment nor the need to correct the structural imbalances which make its perpetuation possible, are a manifestation of this. Such concepts contrast with those of the 1970s and 1980s—the "new international economic order," "basic needs," or "trade not aid"—which, however ideologically flawed, at least implied that some form of more equitable redistributive justice in North-South relations was at hand or called for. At that time, the banner of development in the UN acted as a powerful rallying point for the Third World, much in the same way as the goal of decolonization had mobilized the previous decades. The mantra of national planning, on which development strategies had been built with the broad consensus of the "three worlds," has been replaced by laissez-faire. It can be argued that the liturgical invocation of sustainable human development and of the role of civil society therein, further encourages the bypassing of the shrinking powers of recipient governments. Most Third World officials, whether or not they subscribe to the theory, are not in a position to resist the pressures to privatize.

Furthermore, the emphasis on market mechanisms and the privatization of aid allows donors, and to some extent Third World governments, to eschew the issue of the failure of past development strategies, a failure in which the governments and elites of North and South are complicit. Finally, the fact that both relief and development assistance, because of their privatization, increasingly bypass and therefore weaken recipient governments is indicative of the increasing marginalization of the development discourse in international relations.

Powerful new forces are rapidly changing the shape of the North-South scene and the context of the debate; "development" no longer seems to be the mobilizing paradigm. A new paradigm has yet to emerge. De facto, the new paradigm may well be a combination of intervention and humanitarian assistance, as in political peace-maintenance.

Humanitarianism: The Next Phase of Capitalism?

For the humanitarians, changes in the international context have been both qualitative and quantitative. The escalation of needs has provoked a quantum leap in the response capacity of the *humanitarian international*. But it is the qualitative changes, in particular the implications of working in conflict situations, that are the major defining factor. Under the simpler regime of the Cold War, the humanitarian actors in internal conflicts were few: only the International Committee of the Red Cross (ICRC) and a handful of NGOs were able to circumvent the sovereignty rule and function in areas controlled by forces hostile to recognized governments. UN agencies were almost exclusively confined to government-held territory, where they operated within or through official channels. Working "cross-border" into rebel territory or "cross-line" in and out of government areas was out of the question. Now working on "both sides" has become the norm rather than the exception, even for the UN. This has subjected UN relief agencies to a host of new problems, ranging from negotiating access for staff and relief commodities with warlords and on occasion hiring armed protection, to working with or alongside the military. Humanitarian space has often been difficult to safeguard. For UN personnel, mostly unaccustomed to conditions outside government frameworks, the learning curve has been steep and the price paid high.

In the messy, violent, and volatile context of internal conflicts, where the ruthless warlord's might has replaced the state's monopoly on violence, the fine line of the humanitarian imperative has become difficult to tread. Concepts such as "impartiality" and "neutrality" are no longer immediately understandable, or even pertinent, when humanitarian assistance is massively manipulated, whether by warlords on the ground or "aidlords" and their political masters. Humanitarians are caught between the temptation to fly forward into politics or retreat backwards into logistics or huddle under the cover of military "humanitarian" interventions.

It can be argued, if present trends continue, that there is an increasing risk the privatization of war and the privatization of relief will mutually reinforce each other. Complex emergencies are first and foremost political crises, and it is no wonder that the humanitarians so often get caught up in politics. It is also understood that in order to save lives they must engage "with" politics. In internal wars, this can result in a difficult balancing act between the operational impartiality of the "political eunuch" ("we are here to save lives, politics is not our business") and the shrewd maneuvering of the "humanitarian prostitute" ("we are ready to compromise so that the aid can get through"). The fact that humanitarian assistance is a business and a market complicates things further: agencies, particularly the newer and smaller ones, have to compete for scarce funds and jockey for position, visibility, and video bites. The day-to-day struggle for survival of contract- and media-hungry NGOs is not necessarily synonymous with political acumen, good management, and accountability, nor with sustainable programs.

Evidence is also mounting that warlords and other de facto entities of governance have learned how to use international humanitarian assistance to their advantage, either directly as a weapon of war, by giving food to fighters, or indirectly by attracting agencies and projects to areas under their control, for example. Some have become talented in mimicking the language and the latest operational fad of the outsiders: local councils, indigenous NGOs, joint committees, and so on. Elsewhere, if foreigners are seen to be undesirable either as witnesses or because of the values that they and their assistance represent, it is easy enough to equate them with the enemy and to scare them away with terror tactics or worse. This is not to say that the aid agencies themselves are not responsible for such animosity. Lack of cultural sensitivity, display of wealth—like cars, trucks, computers, or satellite phones—in the midst of extreme poverty, aggressive or directive behavior, and the lack of visible results can all contribute to a climate of reciprocal misunderstanding.[11] From Chechnya to Rwanda, recent events have shown how delicate and dangerous an enterprise humanitarian action can be. Humanitarian workers have paid a high and unacceptable price, a problem made worse by the absence of any protection or recourse system for gross violations of humanitarian law. Sadly, from Afghanistan to Zaire, no individual responsible for the death of a humanitarian worker has ever been identified, tried, or punished.

The humanitarian community is itself rapidly evolving. While many of its members are engaged in constructive debate on how to meet the challenges of working in conflict and chaos, others, for now on the fringe, are rushing into new dimensions. Privatization is spewing "for-profit NGOs" and attendant trade fairs and marketing strategies. While "cowboy NGOs" have always existed, the multiplication of small "truck-by-night NGOs" ready to flock Goma or Gorazde with a maximum of activism and a minimum of experience deserves to be noted. Perhaps, if the experience of aid agencies in Somalia is any indication, the next logical step in the deregulated aid market is the "Mad Max NGO" with a military wing that will ensure access to victims, especially in war zones where the international community is unwilling or unable to intervene. Militarization and privatization have already become frequent bedfellows: private security firms, such as Executive Outcomes in Sierra Leone, will provide, for a price, the conditions for business pursuits to resume;[12] others, like Gurkha Security Guards (involved in demining in Mozambique), are working closely with humanitarian agencies. It is not unlikely that such rapprochement between "mercenaries" of the humanitarian and military varieties will continue.

The next questions that must be asked are: Who profits from extreme poverty? Who pays the bill? What roles is humanitarian assistance, directly or indirectly, being asked to play? The changes in the context and in the manner in which humanitarian assistance is being provided suggest that new tasks are being thrust on, or being voluntarily accepted by, relief agencies. These should be considered in the context of globalization of the economy and privatization of international social safety nets, aid, and relief, on the one hand, and of the international community's reluctance to address the root causes of complex emergencies—whether economic, social, or political—on the other. If humanitarian assistance is asked to fill the political and developmental vacuum at the periphery of the system, does it not itself become political action in its own right? If it is used, more or less systematically, as bandaid, alibi, or smoke screen, does this not corrupt the very nature of the humanitarian imperative?

Some hard thinking is in order to better define the true functions of humanitarian assistance in contemporary crises. This in turn should inform the debate on the changing nature of humanitarianism. Containment, appeasement, keeping conflict within state boundaries, and stanching the flow of refugees have all become key goals. Humanitarian assistance does not address the problems of extreme poverty; it tends to become a palliative that prevents instability from spinning out of control. It has become the preferred response of the international community when it is unable or unwilling to face the fact that the quantum of political will at its disposal is woefully inadequate. It prefers relief, precisely, to soothe the pain, because it cannot look at the causes. And, as the latter are neither understood nor addressed, crises appear to be intractable.

With the demise of the state-to-state aid regime, and the corresponding weakening of state structures in the South, international governance has been reduced to a basic security function. Humanitarian assistance and the globalization of the capitalist model are not unconnected. Could it be that the former creates the space for the latter to thrive? The unbridled pursuit of profit in countries in crisis seems to have fueled their wars and created massive humanitarian needs. For example, more than $300 million worth of diamonds are exported annually from Liberia; a single warlord, according to one estimate, was reaping some $400 million per year.[13] As such, does the corporate sector, and in particular those legitimate private companies that have derived direct benefit from the illegitimate plundering of national resources, not have a responsibility to contribute towards reconstruction? If it does not, can humanitarian assistance continue to turn a blind eye to the external ramifications of internal disputes?

Furthermore, as insecurity mounts and institutions of governance break down, "official" public and private development projects and private investment funds are naturally the first to disappear from conflict zones. What is less clear is how the economy continues to function and what distortions occur. Two trends seem to emerge: the criminalization of the economy—including drug trafficking and arms smuggling to supply the war effort—and the emergence of warlord-affiliated private enterprises connected through proxies to the global markets.[14] In the first case, national resources—like the diamonds in Liberia and Sierra Leone or timber in Cambodia—are being squandered to sustain the fighting. In the second, private capital is taking advantage of the breakdown of law and order.

War becomes a business: in both cases, the privatization of war and the privatization of national resources seem to go hand-in-hand. In the most extreme cases, these resources are being mortgaged in order to pay for the security provided by private "venture capital" operations, of the Executive Outcomes kind. Business, itself, is also war: it is no secret, for example, that one of the stakes in the Afghan civil war is control of the corridor for the oil and gas pipeline leading from Central Asia to the

Indian Ocean. The geopolitics of oil may be in fact driving the fighting, the objective being to secure this territory in Afghanistan before the Iranian corridor becomes a viable alternative. The fact that huge profits are being reaped or planned by "reputable" enterprises is a manifestation of how humanitarian crises are linked to the globalization of the world economy.

The Political Economy of Peace

The strains of working in ill-defined and volatile conditions have generated widespread "unease" in the humanitarian community.[15] There is a responsibility to redefine "humanitarianism" by recognizing that the contexts in which aid agencies operate are eminently political, and so are the uses to which they are put. The obligation to save lives remains intact. But there is no obligation to remain blindfolded. Humanitarian space (which ensures access and protected delivery) and humanitarian time (which demands timeliness of action—and its forward and backward linkages to politics and development) will need constant redefinition in order to minimize unintended negative impacts. Principles will have to be upheld, safeguarded, and placed up front. For instance, had we made it clear in Afghanistan, years ago, that the UN "stands for principles"—rather than agreeing to compromise with disreputable groups so that the assistance could get through (or worse, closing our eyes to human rights violations)— we would not have been caught napping by the Taliban today on the issue of women's rights.[16] And the humanitarian "trade" will need to be better policed in order to ensure greater effectiveness and accountability.

A "politically alert" approach may well lead to the demise of humanitarianism as we know it: justice and solidarity, rather than impartiality and neutrality, might well become the watchwords. There are obvious risks in an approach that puts the political dimension at center stage; but then there are perhaps major risks involved in attachment to the purist "operational-neutrality" approach. Even the historical custodian of principles, the ICRC, is rethinking its role in complex crises after having been directly targeted, particularly in Chechnya. Such alertness is perhaps the precondition for a strategic and holistic understanding of conflicts and for the orchestrating of an appropriate response, whether political, humanitarian, or developmental, on the basis of clearly defined and understood ethical principles.

There is now widespread acknowledgment that saving lives is not enough. Planting the seeds for the reconstruction of livelihoods is obviously better, but it is easier said than done in the midst of violence and the continuing erosion of human rights and humanitarian norms. Conventional wisdom has it that if we addressed the causes, emergencies would disappear like morning mist. The political economy of peacemaking is not so simple: we must engage with the causes and the consequences at the same time. Dealing separately with the political, economic, and humanitarian dimensions can sometimes provide breathing space for the international community but rarely leads to durable and sustainable solutions. The challenge, therefore, once the context of the crisis and its external ramifications are better understood, is to develop a comprehensive strategic framework for peace-maintenance and beyond. In most cases, this will require the international community to funnel its efforts through a "center of gravity"—as described by Richard Cousens in the next chapter—which will provide both a coherent multifunctional approach and a sufficient critical mass of resources capable of ensuring that the logic of peace will overwhelm the logic of war.

Conclusion

The following points are advanced as part of the debate on how the humanitarian dimension might contribute to operationalizing the concept of peace-maintenance articulated in this volume.

The three cultures. During internal conflict, as in Bosnia and Somalia, the humanitarian and peace agendas do not necessarily coincide, and the development agenda is nowhere on the radar screen. Advantages and disadvantages of separation, insulation, and integration of the political, humanitarian, and recovery processes must be carefully weighed. However, when peace is in sight (at the very latest), and earlier if possible, an integrated vision and strategy become key.

Conflicts are not aberrations in the linear process of development. The roots of violent competition are in the politics and economics of the society. These can be exacerbated by external manipulation or, for example, by the "inadvertent" effects of internationally supported structural adjustment programs—in addition to the "advertent" effects of divisive political action and warlordism. Similarly, recovery is not linear; it does not start where development stopped. As well as human, social, and economic destruction, conflicts can create huge structural imbalances. A conflict-ridden economy cannot be pumped up like a deflated balloon.

We may have to consider ways of doing rehabilitation, recovery, and development work and reviving the economy during wartime as part of a peace-maintenance strategy (since in criminalized economies it is unlikely that key actors will forgo warlordism in the absence of economic alternatives). We have understood that it is necessary to plan for recovery while battles still continue, but we have as yet little experience in sharpening the tools to do so. Recent decisions in the UN system and in the secretary-general's reform package are encouraging steps in this direction.[17] The Administrative Committee on Coordination (ACC), for instance, has decided to engage in a system-wide strategic framework exercise in two countries in crisis or recovering from crisis—Afghanistan and Mozambique.

Institutional emergencies. In addition to being *humanitarian* emergencies and *development* emergencies, countries in conflict and crisis are also *institutional* emergencies. They are "emergencies of *governance*" because the structures of government all but disappear, and traditional coping mechanisms and local civil society patterns are deeply affected. Internal conflict destroys the social fabric, the glue that keeps society together. Healing the wounds means much more than injecting money into the economy and rebuilding institutions. The legacy of conflict continues for many years. Land mines may kill for decades. But the hidden traumas of war also need to be addressed. We have little experience in dealing with fifteen-year-olds who have never been to school but are proficient in using assault rifles as a coping mechanism. The costs of replacing a culture of war with a culture of peace are formidable. It is a sad realization that one or even two generations may be lost in the process. UN peace missions follow a strict timetable and often result in a "vote-and-forget" syndrome. There is no option but to mobilize the necessary resources to help this process along. But recovery from crisis will fail unless it is "illuminated from within."

The long haul. Intractable situations—in the Great Lakes region of central Africa, for example—will remain intractable if we continue to apply outdated recipes. The private sector has already been more innovative: Executive Outcomes has brought peace (of sorts) to Sierra Leone in exchange for a mortgage on the country's natural resources; and the Unocal Corporation plans to build a pipeline through western Afghanistan and provide humanitarian assistance in order to keep the peace on its way. Rather than spending $1 million worth of relief each day to contain the seemingly insoluble problem of the Great Lakes, the international community might be wise to resort to the audacity of the private sector or to revert to that of the victors of World War II. Outrageous ideas should be explored, such as "land for peace for development" under an overall "blue umbrella," as aptly recommended by Jarat Chopra in his introduction. This would imply, for instance, a political agreement that might include a ninety-nine-year "UN lease" on parts of the Democratic Republic of the Congo (formerly Zaire) and Tanzania, in order to resettle the displaced on the basis of organized population movements, and a Marshall Plan and/or an economic integration program for the Great Lakes region. Interestingly, the UN and Organization of African Unity (OAU) special representatives for the Great Lakes have called repeatedly for a "mini Marshall Plan." As Chopra stresses, such an approach is the contrary of colonization; it is more in the nature of a political and economic contract guaranteed by the international community in its entirety. This would give real meaning to the hollow slogan of "preventive development." It would also show that the costs of inaction, in the long term, are vastly greater than the costs of forward-looking action.

The vision thing. All else having failed, "vision" may well be the only and the most cost-effective solution left. There is sore need for a strategic and holistic approach to conflicts that generate extreme suffering and poverty, and for orchestrating the response, whether political, humanitarian, or developmental, on the basis of clear ethical principles. The new theory will of course require a new practice: UN agencies, regional institutions, donors, and implementing partners on the ground will have to work together to develop joint strategies for such a response and to ensure a positive relationship between relief and development. A more unitary, managed approach, built around a single UN administrator (rather than a coordinator) of all UN efforts in a particular country, coupled with a strong strategic framework for reconstruction, bringing together the UN humanitarian and development agencies, the financial institutions, and the donor community, is likely to be required. It will be necessary to move beyond the traditional concepts of "coordination" of international assistance in appreciation of the fact that in "emergencies of governance," where counterpart institutions are weak or nonexistent, the UN must play a much stronger role and even assume "surrogate government functions," until such time as more legitimate or recognized national institutions are in a position to take over. The weaker the state, the stronger the UN role is likely to be.[18]

Given the current culture in the UN and the vested interests of all the key actors in the international community, the obstacles are likely to be formidable. But the cost of inaction will undoubtedly be much higher: spreading conflict and anarchy of Kaplanesque proportions will soon threaten the stability of the entrenched capitalist citadel.

There can be no missing links in peace-maintenance: political, humanitarian, social, and material reconstruction needs have to be addressed at the same time. If one element is left out of the equation—whether demobilization and reintegration of soldiers or the reform of the judiciary—then the whole peace process is compromised. Herein lies the challenge of peace-maintenance. As Dutch development minister Jan Pronk is wont to say: we cannot wait for development "until it is safe."[19] We cannot wait for peace in order to start reconstruction. We must take conflict for granted and integrate humanitarian action and development with politics. ⊕

Notes

Antonio Donini is chief of the lessons learned unit of the United Nations Department of Humanitarian Affairs (UNDHA). He was formerly a senior officer in the executive office of the UN Secretary-General and a staff member of the joint inspection unit. From 1989 to 1991, he served with the UN Office for the Coordination of Humanitarian Assistance to Afghanistan (UNOCA), and was deputy chief of mission in Islamabad and chief of mission in Kabul. Views are expressed in a personal capacity and are not to be attributed to UNDHA.

1. See Rakiya Omaar and Alex de Waal, *Humanitarianism Unbound? Current Dilemmas Facing Multi-Mandate Relief Operations in Political Emergencies* (London: African Rights, November 1994). The ethical debate is summarized in Joanna Macrae, "The Origins of Unease," unpublished paper presented at a seminar on "Ethics in Humanitarian Aid," Dublin, 9–10 December 1996.

2. See the recommendations contained in the Synthesis Report of the multi-donor evaluation of emergency assistance to Rwanda, John Eriksson et al., *The International Response to Conflict and Genocide: Lessons from the Rwandan Experience*, vol. 5 (Copenhagen: Steering Committee of the Joint Evaluation of Emergency Assistance to Rwanda, March 1996). Among the spate of publications issued in conjunction with the fiftieth anniversary of the UN, see Erskine Childers with Brian Urquhart, *Renewing the United Nations System* (Uppsala: Dag Hammarskjöld Foundation, 1994), where the authors argue for a consolidation of the UN system relief agencies—including UNHCR, WFP, and UNICEF—into a single entity. Similar proposals have been made by: Gareth Evans in *Cooperating for Peace: The Global Agenda for the 1990s and Beyond* (St. Leonards, N.S.W: Allen & Unwin, 1993), pp. 178–179; Oxfam in a paper circulated in January 1995 (and now reposted in the electronic *Journal of Humanitarian Assistance*, Cambridge University, http://www-jha.sps.cam.ac.uk); and in a "nonpaper" distributed by the U.S. delegation at ECOSOC in July 1995. A more radical proposal for the "internationalization" of ICRC or for the creation of a separate, non-UN organization, for the provision of emergency relief was made by James Ingram, former head of WFP, "The Future Architecture for International Humanitarian Assistance," in Thomas G. Weiss and Larry Minear, eds., *Humanitarianism Across Borders: Sustaining Civilians in Times of War* (Boulder: Lynne Rienner, 1994), pp. 171–193.

3. Martin van Creveld, *On Future War* (London: Brassey's, 1991); David Keen and Ken Wilson, "Engaging with Violence: A Reassessment of the Role of Relief in Wartime," in Joanna Macrae and Anthony Zwi, *War and Hunger: Rethinking International Responses to Complex Emergencies* (London: Zed Press, 1994), pp. 209–222.

4. Compare Larry Minear and Philippe Guillot, *Soldiers to the Rescue: Humanitarian Lessons from Rwanda* (Paris: Organisation for Economic Cooperation and Development, 1996).

5. See further, Antonio Donini, *The Policies of Mercy: UN Coordination in Afghanistan, Mozambique, and Rwanda* (Providence, R.I.: Thomas J. Watson Jr. Institute for International Studies, 1996), pp. 77–80; compare Peter Uvin and Isabelle Biagiotti, "Global Governance and the 'New' Political Conditionality," *Global Governance* 2, no. 3 (September-December 1996): 377–400.

6. See further, Mark Duffield, "NGO relief in war zones: towards an analysis of the new aid paradigm," *Third World Quarterly* 18, no. 3 (1997): 527–542; Antonio Donini, "The bureaucracy and the free spirits: stagnation and innovation in the relationship between the UN and NGOs," *Third World Quarterly* 16, no. 3 (September 1995): 421–439.

7. This "New Partnership Initiative" was announced by U.S. vice-president Al Gore in his statement at the World Summit for Social Development, Copenhagen, March 1995. See Barbara Crossette, "Gore Says U.S. Will Shift More Foreign Aid To Private Groups," *The New York Times*, 13 March 1995, p. A7.

8. UNDHA estimates based on U.S. State Department data, February 1997.

9. Compare Ian Smillie, "NGOs and development assistance: a change in mind-set?" *Third World Quarterly* 18, no. 3 (1997): 563–577.

10. Compare Peter Uvin, *Development, Aid and Conflict: Reflections from the Case of Rwanda* (Helsinki: United Nations University (UNU)/World Institute for Development Economics Research (WIDER), 1996).

11. For more on the "white car syndrome," see the lessons learned report by Antonio Donini, Eric Dudley, and Ron Ockwell, *Afghanistan: Coordination in a Fragmented State* (New York: United Nations Department of Humanitarian Affairs, December 1996), pp. 41–42.

· 12. William Reno, "Humanitarian Emergencies and Warlord Politics in Liberia and Sierra Leone," paper presented to the WIDER conference on "The Political Economy of Humanitarian Emergencies", Helsinki, 6–8 October 1996; and "Privatizing War in Sierra Leone," *Current History* 96, no. 610 (May 1997): 227–230. On Executive Outcomes in Sierra Leone, see also Elizabeth Rubin, "An Army of One's Own," *Harper's Magazine* (February 1997): 44–55. On this practice by the United States, see Ken Silverstein, "Privatizing War: How Affairs of State are Outsourced to Corporations Beyond Public Control," *The Nation* (28 July–4 August 1997): 11–17.

13. Cited in Reno, "Humanitarian Emergencies."

14. François Jean and Jean-Cristophe Rufin, *Economie des guerres civiles* (Paris: Hachette, 1996).

15. See Macrae, "The Origins of Unease."

16. Donini et al., *Afghanistan*, pp. 39–41.

17. For Secretary-General Kofi Annan's reform proposals, see "Renewing the United Nations: Programme for Reform," UN Doc. A/51/1950 of 16 July 1997.

18. The possible elements of a more unitary approach to the UN's involvements in weak or fragmented states is described in Donini et al., *Afghanistan*, pp. 42–50. The strategic framework for recovery and reconstruction, and the preconditions for operationalizing it, are currently being discussed in various UN fora, in particular in the Consultative Committee on Program and Operational questions (see the consultant's report prepared by Hugh Cholmondeley, "The Role of the United Nations System in Post-Conflict Recovery," Doc. ACC/1996/POQ/CPP 16 Rev of 20 September 1996).

19. Statement by Jan Pronk, minister of development cooperation of the Netherlands at the UNHCR/IPA Conference on "Healing the Wounds: Refugees, Reconstruction and Reconciliation," Princeton University, July 1996.

6

Providing Military Security
in Peace-Maintenance

———————— ⊕ ————————

Richard P. Cousens

❝The general's first duty is to win his nation's battles."[1] Though many might yearn for custom-designed forces for deployment on a variety of military peace-support operations, the sad fact remains that most armies are structured, organized, and trained for war. History indicates that there is unlikely to be any change to this primary focus. Therefore, military forces deployed in support of political peace-maintenance will be required to adjust their structures to conform with the mission, but not their culture nor the manner in which command and decisionmaking are exercised. The intellectual analysis of a mission is likely to be the same regardless of the nature of the task, and there are certain overarching concepts and disciplines that will govern the manner in which a military commander will approach that task.

These methods are the product of experience, history, and the impact of technology. They are not the characteristics of a blinkered, traditional, and inflexible culture, but rather processes that foster rapid decisionmaking, devolution to junior commanders, and an acceptance of a certain degree of risk. The core of this chapter addresses how the military commander is likely to think and what the expectations might be from other senior, civilian representatives within a multiagency peace-maintenance operation. Above all, it acknowledges that the military commander might not, and indeed should not, be the overall commander of the mission; but certain principles, proven in past campaigns, are worthy of explanation and might illuminate the path to success.

Warfighting

British defense policy is typical when illustrating why armed forces are generally not custom-designed for peace support operations and why units embarking on any of the four categories of peace-maintenance—whether *assistance*, *partnership*, *control*, or *governorship*—will probably be doing so by deviating from their primary role. They may well be extremely proficient, but they will not exist exclusively for deployment on peace-maintenance operations. The stated goal of British defense policy is "to maintain the freedom and territorial integrity of the United Kingdom and its Dependent Territories, and the ability to pursue its legitimate interests at home and abroad."[2] The policy is defined in terms of three overlapping roles: (1) the protection and security of the U.K., even when there is no external threat; (2) insurance against a major external threat to the U.K. and her allies; and (3) contributing to promotion of the U.K.'s wider security interests through the maintenance of international peace and stability. Hence, peace-maintenance tasks are likely to be performed under the aegis of the third defense role.

For example, two U.K. divisions are assigned to the Allied Command Europe Rapid Reaction Corps (ARRC), the headquarters of which recently exercised military command in Bosnia. Formed in October 1992, ARRC maintains a high state of readiness and constitutes the main land component of the North Atlantic Treaty Organization's (NATO's) rapid reaction capability. It is multinational, bringing together the armies of twelve nations, and can deploy with up to four of the ten divisions assigned to it. It has proved to be an excellent structure for command of multinational forces in Bosnia, but it exists to fight at the highest end of the conflict spectrum and is configured accordingly; it does not exist solely to conduct peace support operations. It is designed for war and its commanders are trained to command and make their decisions in war.

Both the U.S. and U.K. armies differentiate between *operations*, or warfighting, and *operations other than war* (OOTW).[3] Any peace-maintenance task is likely to fall within the OOTW category, with the implicit potential for the task to escalate into full military *operations*. British doctrine acknowledges only three types of OOTW: peace support operations, counterinsurgency operations, and limited intervention, such as a services-protected evacuation from an overseas territory. U.S. doctrine, on the other hand, acknowledges thirteen separate types of operation within the OOTW category, and this distinction perhaps reflects the differences in culture and history of the two armies. In both cases, as with most armies, U.S. *peace* operations or U.K. *peace support* operations lie within OOTW, and consequently peace-maintenance tasks are likely to be approached from the same doctrinal standpoint.

Having acknowledged that peace-maintenance tasks will not affect core structures, it is important to explain that commanders will approach such tasks just as they would in warfighting. They will expect a cohesive campaign plan linked to strategic goals and unity of command regardless of the number of agencies. They will expect an exit strategy based on success and not time and, being historians, will know that any OOTW task can be measured in years and not months. They will be aware that successful joint operations with all agencies provide the key to success; they will have studied the failure of operations in which military contingents operated in a vacuum. They will also long for a well-defined chain of command, with timely decisionmaking taking place in the theater of operations. They will have been schooled in the significance of the operational level of command, a level that is rarely acknowledged by politicians, UN functionaries, or academics. They will know that the success of the campaigns in Malaysia, Borneo, Oman, and Rhodesia-Zimbabwe reflected vision and clarity at the operational level, in which military tasks were integrated with social, economic, cultural, and even agricultural dimensions.

Operational Art and Peace-Maintenance

The main dimensions of providing military security within any category of peace-maintenance are associated with the successful application of operational art. Indeed, arguably, without an understanding of operational art, any form of peace-maintenance is doomed. "Operational Art is the skilful employment of military forces to attain strategic goals through the design, organisation, integration and conduct of campaigns and major operations."[4] In essence, operational art requires a commander, any commander, to identify the conditions, or "end-state," that constitute success and that will thus mirror the strategic objective. Field Marshal Viscount William Slim referred to this as the necessity to "think big"; that is, to consider all dimensions and not be tempted to muddle through. Field Marshall Viscount Bernard Montgomery stated the problem with typical succinctness: "It is essential to relate what is strategically desirable to what is tactically possible with the forces at your disposal. To this end it is necessary to decide the development of operations before the initial blow is delivered."[5] Though blows are hardly likely to be appropriate in peace-maintenance, the principle of decisiveness remains valid but has rarely been applied in any peace support operation since 1988. Muddling through has been the order of the day.

   Successful application of operational art assumes a clear understanding of the various levels of command. At the strategic end of the spectrum, British doctrine differentiates between the grand strategic and military strategic levels. It describes grand strategy as "the application of national resources to achieve policy objectives," which will invariably include diplomatic and economic resources.[6] Military strategy, on the other hand, is "the application of military resources to achieve grand strategic objectives."[7] But it is the operational level that determines success or failure. U.K. and U.S. doctrine concur in this area. U.S. doctrine describes the operational level as "pivotal to the planning, conduct and sustainment of campaigns. It provides the context for tactical planning and decision making. . . . It is at this level that the sequence of activities occurs that produces military actions that link the tactical employment of forces to the strategic objectives of the campaign."[8] U.K. doctrine refers to it as "the level that provides the gearing between . . . strategic objectives and all tactical activity in the theatre of operations."9

Given the significance of the operational level, it is necessary to focus on the operational level commander and his responsibilities. It is probably inappropriate for a military officer to be the true operational level commander in any peace-maintenance mission. The fusion of the many agencies concerned is unlikely to be accomplished by a soldier, though it has been achieved in some past counterinsurgency campaigns. As Andy Knight argues above, choice of the lead individual and agency will be dictated by their unifying capability and multifunctional knowledge and experience. Selection also depends on the nature of the operational end-state and its relationship to the strategic end-state. In the U.S. and British armies, commanders are appointed on the basis of merit and would be prepared to lead both in warfighting and on peace operations. Similarly, civilian leaders must be credible and capable of achieving the mission objectives. Politicization of posts dangerously threatens a successful outcome.

Whether in uniform or safari suit, the operational commander, properly advised by experts, is charged with designing a campaign within a delegated theater of operations and subsequently with directing the major operations within that campaign. The commander has five main tasks: (1) to decide what tactical objectives (civil as well as military) are necessary to achieve the campaign objectives; (2) to decide the sequence of these activities; (3) to allocate the necessary resources to subordinate executives, so that the activities may be accomplished; (4) to identify priorities for logistic and administrative support; and (5) to direct all those activities not devolved to subordinate commanders. Muddling through is not an option.

At risk of alarming the nongovernmental organization worker with a natural antipathy to all things military, there is a clear link between the successful application of operational art in any form of peace-maintenance and that applied in counterinsurgency operations. Many of the factors are the same in that success is related to people, perceptions, and ideas rather than to the mere application of overwhelming military force—as Clement Adibe emphasizes in the next chapter. In an article on military doctrine and counterinsurgency, Gavin Bulloch goes to the heart of the matter: "The military plan should form one strand in a coordinated 'attack.'. . . This should be established by a strategic estimate [analysis] conducted by a government taking military and other advice. From this will flow further operational and tactical estimates and plans. While military forces may have a critical role to play at certain stages in the campaign, overall their contribution will be secondary and should be kept in perspective."10 Bulloch's remarks also reflect the difference between a traditional "attritionalist" approach and the more favored "maneuverist" theory; the former places undue emphasis on military responses, while the latter respects the intellectual and psychological aspects of operations and not just the hardware.

Peace-Maintenance Campaign Planning

Potentially the most significant ingredient for the successful use of military forces in peace-maintenance is a coherent campaign plan, in which "muddling through" receives no mention. Associated concepts are complex and it is beyond the scope of this chapter to explain them fully. However, it is important to convey a flavor of some of the ideas concerned. U.S. doctrine refers to these as *doctrinal elements of operational art,* whereas British doctrine describes them as *concepts of operational design.*[11] They are broadly the same and the key elements identical. They include such concepts as the end-state, center of gravity, decisive points, lines of operation, sequencing, contingency planning, and tempo. The concept of "end-state" is generally well understood, but some of the others are worth considering to underline the importance of operational art in peace-maintenance and to avoid the natural temptation to muddle through.

Identification of the *center of gravity* is, perhaps, the most critical analytical step in the design of a campaign plan at the strategic and operational levels. A center of gravity is often difficult to define. For example, at the strategic level it might be as abstract as public opinion, whereas at the operational level it might be the cohesion of factions within the country concerned. However difficult it might be to identify, there is a tangible link between the strategic center of gravity, operational objectives, the operational center of gravity, and—eventually—success. Some counterinsurgency campaigns offer good examples of the process. The Dhofar campaign within Oman illustrated the key role that the political interface and civil affairs may play in defining military operational centers of gravity. "The promises of the insurgents—improved living conditions for the population—were in the event delivered first by the Sultan's Armed Forces, thereby cutting the ground from under the insurgents' feet and isolating them from the people."[12] Though initially a counterinsurgency operation, it could be argued that the Dhofar campaign transitioned to an *assistance* category of peace-maintenance. It has been studied in depth at the British Army Staff College, Camberley, because it was a success and because many of the lessons, principles, and procedures at the operational as well as the tactical levels are enduring and timeless.

After successfully identifying the center of gravity, the campaign planner needs to construct a coherent plan, which respects that center of gravity and which leads to a successful end-state. This will be arrived at not by accident but by design. Thus, the planner is likely to identify certain *decisive points*, or those events the successful outcome of which is a precondition to addressing the center of gravity. These, in turn, are linked by *lines of operation*, which establish the relationship between decisive points and ensure that events are tackled in a logical sequence. They represent stepping stones that should be placed in order toward the desired end-state and, as no plan is likely to survive initial deployment, the stones can be adjusted by building into the plan an anticipation of opportunities and reverses. This process is called *contingency planning* and should be the product of rigorous analysis and not a knee-jerk reaction to the unexpected.

Civil-Military Relations

The coherence of the campaign plan being the pivotal ingredient for the effective employment of military forces in peace-maintenance, the second factor that will have a critical influence on the successful outcome of an operation is the whole question of civil-military relations. So often this has gone horribly wrong, with mutual suspicion and even antagonism developing between military elements and the various civilian agencies, particularly humanitarian organizations, which Antonio Donini describes in his chapter. The causes are generally the same: confusion caused by a foggy command chain, competition, and military forces preferring to operate in isolation. Peace-maintenance operations, of whichever category, will be a corporate effort geared, with luck, to a coherent campaign plan, and thus the manner in which military force and civil agencies interrelate will be critical. The process is complicated and John McCuen, writing on counterinsurgency, addresses the problem:

> Unified planning, centralised control, and a single point of responsibility are the very minimum requirements for a unity of effort which will offer success. . . . Unity of effort, however, is extremely difficult to achieve because it represents the fusion of civil and military functions to fight battles which have primarily political objectives. . . . All the political, economic, psychological, and military means must be marshalled as weapons under centralised co-ordination and direction. Unity of effort can be achieved by a single commander as the French advocate. Unity of effort can be achieved by a committee, under civilian leadership, as the British advocate.[13]

This committee system merits further review, for it has been refined over the years and it works. It is deeply embedded in British doctrine and is reflected in how the civil and military forces relate in Northern Ireland. Frank Kitson has written extensively on the subject and describes it: "Under this system a committee would be formed at every level on which would sit the senior military officer and police officers for the area under the chairmanship of the head administrator. The committee might co-opt members representing other interests, and it would be served by officials. . . . Decisions would be taken jointly and implemented by the members using the organisations or units under their command."[14]

The need for a mechanism whereby the civil and military authorities work in tandem has been acknowledged for many years and, during counterrevolutionary operations, was further refined. The mechanism in the

1960s and 1970s included a national defense council at the strategic level and a national operations committee at the operational level. The latter was chaired by an individual known as the director of operations, who was responsible for the campaign and was not necessarily a military officer. All acknowledged, military and civilian, that there was only one individual responsible for the direction of operations and that a structure existed, as a series of subordinate *operations committees*, through which all civil and military activities could be planned, agreed on, and synchronized.

Military commanders are unlikely to call the shots in any form of peace-maintenance; subordination to a civil authority is likely to be the norm. In *assistance*, the role of military forces is likely to be low-key, in order to gently foster existing structures. Small military training teams might be deployed to help train, equip, and organize the local armed forces, so that they become proficient and operate within the law. Such missions have been successfully accomplished in Uganda, Zimbabwe, and South Africa. In *partnership*, the role of military forces is likely to be more subtle and might even involve the establishment of a staff college, so that senior officers and opinion-formers might be properly trained to run their own military forces. This has worked well in certain countries in the Middle East and a genuine partnership between armed forces has been achieved, as well as a unity of doctrine.

Both *control* and *governorship* imply surrender of a degree of national executive authority and therefore, in these categories, the provision of military security is likely to be much more comprehensive and, consequently, complicated. The operation is likely to resemble existing peace support missions, in that the force structures required will be generally similar. An independent military force, deployed in an expeditionary manner, will need to be self-sufficient and will be structured to include headquarters, maneuver units, transport, and logistics. As in existing peace support operations, engineers will continue to perform particularly important tasks, since not only can they support the force, but they can also be employed on projects associated with the improvement of the infrastructure of the country concerned—a form of peace-building that can affect the daily lives of the local population, again as Adibe advocates. The difference within these two categories of peace-maintenance should lie in the manner in which the forces are commanded and the coherence of the plan. Muddling through has been a regular feature of "wider peacekeeping" operations; it is not an option in any form of peace-maintenance.

Conclusion

Far-reaching changes in docrine relating to peace support operations have taken place throughout the decade and, arguably, the catalyst for this dynamic evolution was the concept of "second-generation multinational operations."[15] Developed by John Mackinlay and Jarat Chopra of Brown University, this concept sparked a reevaluation of traditional peacekeeping doctrine, which had become somewhat sterile, and served to readdress the subject in a new international scene. In 1994, the British army published its field manual *Wider Peacekeeping*, which reflects many of the concepts in the original Brown University project; and, after extensive debate, the U.S. army produced field manual 100–23, *Peace Operations*. Even more significantly, it has been recognized that peace operations are joint in nature; they involve the participation of navies and air forces as well as armies and, consequently, joint doctrine is beginning to emerge. The U.S. Joint Warfighting Center at Fort Monroe, Virginia—probably the leading authority on joint doctrine—published *The Joint Task Force Commander's Handbook for Peace Operations* in 1995 as well as other manuals that are wholly appropriate to peace-maintenance.

Much has been written on key topics, such as the significance of consent, rules of engagement (ROE), and the use of force. It is in this latter area that most divergence has been apparent, and Richard Smith has addressed the various approaches reflected in British, French, and American doctrine. He stresses that "at the heart of a common doctrine should be the guiding principle of the use of minimum force, as evolved in the British experience of Low Intensity Conflict, rather than the more restrictive concept of self-defence. The basis of this principle is that the minimum necessary force should be applied to achieve the immediate military aim proportional to the threat."[16]

The evolution of peace-maintenance would not require a widespread reevaluation of doctrine but actually reflects the ideals of existing high level doctrine in most armies. The political constraints remain huge and are addressed elsewhere but, in pure doctrinal terms, the four categories of peace-maintenance require no huge cultural shift by a military commander. On the contrary, it is a concept that aims to focus the minds of those at the strategic and operational levels and offers a real alternative to muddling through. ⊕

Notes

Col. Richard P. Cousens, OBE, is the U.K. Liaison Officer to the U.S. Training and Doctrine Command (TRADOC) at Fort Monroe, Virginia. He is an expert in campaign planning and was formerly an instructor and divisional colonel at the U.K. Staff College in Camberley, England. The opinions expressed are the author's own and should not be taken as an expression of official British government policy.

1. Alistair Irwin, "The Buffalo Thorn: The nature of the future battlefield," *Journal of Strategic Studies* 19, no. 4 (December 1996): 227.

2. Directorate of Defence Policy, Ministry of Defence, *Statement on the Defence Estimates 1996* (London: Her Majesty's Stationery Office, May 1996), p. 3, par. 101.

3. U.S. Army Field Manual 100–5, *Operations* (Washington, D.C.: Headquarters, Department of the Army, 1993), chap. 13; and *Operations*, vol. 1 of U.K. Army Doctrine Publication, (London: Headquarters, Doctrine and Training, Ministry of Defence, June 1994), chap. 7, which refers to OOTWs as "operations short of war."

4. U.K. Army Doctrine Publication, *Operations*, p. 3.1, par. 0301.

5. Slim and Montgomery are quoted in Ibid., p. 3.1 and p. 3.2, respectively. See also William R. Slim, *Defeat into Victory* (London: Cassell, 1956).

6. U.K. Army Doctrine Publication, *Operations*, p. 3.2, par. 0303.

7. Ibid.

8. U.S. Joint Publication 5-00.1, *Joint Tactics, Techniques, and Procedures for Campaign Planning* (Fort Monroe, Va.: Joint Warfighting Center, 30 November 1985), p. I.6.

9. U.K. Army Doctrine Publication, *Operations*, p. 3.4, par. 0308.

10. Gavin Bulloch, "Military Doctrine and Counterinsurgency: A British Perspective," *Parameters* 26, no. 2, (summer 1996): 8.

11. U.S. Joint Publication 5–00.1, *Joint Tactics, Techniques, and Procedures for Campaign Planning,* p. III.3; and U.K. Army Doctrine Publication, *Operations,* p. 3.8, par. 0324.

12. U.K. Army Doctrine Publication, *Operations*, p. 3.12, par. 0331.

13. John J. McCuen, *The Art of Counter-Revolutionary War* (London: Faber & Faber, 1966), pp. 72–73.

14. Frank Kitson, *Low-Intensity Operations* (London: Faber & Faber, 1971), p. 54.

15. John Mackinlay and Jarat Chopra, *A Draft Concept of Second Generation Multinational Operations 1993* (Providence, R.I.: Thomas J. Watson Jr. Institute for International Studies, 1993).

16. Richard Smith, *The Requirement for the United Nations to Develop an Internationally Recognized Doctrine for the Use of Force in Intra-State Conflict* (Camberley, England: Strategic and Combat Studies Institute, 1994), pp. 39–40.

7

Accepting External Authority in Peace-Maintenance

⊕

Clement E. Adibe

A direct relationship exists between the failure of existing approaches to conflict resolution by the UN and current considerations of the notion of "peace-maintenance."[1] If the UN Protection Force (UN-PROFOR) in the former Yugoslavia and the UN Operation in Somalia (UNO-SOM) had not been such miserable and conspicuous disasters, the focus of diplomats and scholars would not have shifted so swiftly to a serious reconsideration of the role of the organization in conflict resolution.[2] Sadly, both missions reflected the flawed logic of bravado that underscored the conception and function of "second-generation" peace operations.[3]

The increasing number of studies and ruminations on the failure of various UN missions tend to focus on the nature of the particular conflicts, the key actors involved, the level of weapons, and the strength, composition, and cohesion of the UN forces dispatched to keep the peace. Missing from these analyses has been any consideration of legitimate authority, the collapse of which *within* the nation-state led to the conflicts in the first place, and the reconstitution of which through *external* assistance has been the very essence of UN peace operations.[4] In this chapter, I shall examine the conditions for accepting UN authority in "collapsed states," as part of a general evaluation of the theory of peace-maintenance. The chapter is divided into three sections. The first examines the concept of authority and its relevance to the theory of peace-maintenance. The next section examines four variables that influence the likelihood a given population will accept UN authority. The final section concludes with some thoughts on bringing people back into any future model of conflict resolution.

Political Authority and the Concept of Peace-Maintenance

Central to the concept of peace-maintenance is the notion of political authority. According to Jarat Chopra in his introduction and elsewhere, the missing element of the conceptual and practical aspects of first- and second-generation peace operations is political authority; that is, the imperative for missions to "fulfil a political, executive function locally if social conditions are to be transformed from violent conflict to a rule of law that can be maintained."[5] What, we might ask, is the relationship between political authority and peace-maintenance? Indeed, why peace-maintenance in the first place? These questions point to the need for contextualization.

An empirical link between the concept of political authority and peace-maintenance may be found, for instance, in Africa. A recent study of the continent by I. William Zartman poses political authority as the kernel of state collapse, the very phenomenon to which UN peace operations have been conceived to respond.[6] "State collapse," writes Zartman, "refers to a situation where the structure, authority (legitimate power), law, and political order have *fallen apart and must be reconstituted* in some form, old or new."[7] This definition is significant for two reasons. First, it captures the essence of the state as "the authoritative political institution" in any society. In this regard, the state is the *accepted* source and symbol of individual identity and the guarantor of security for the population.[8] Second, Zartman's definition *assumes* the necessity to reconstitute the state, should it fall apart. This assumption forms the basis of past and current UN efforts in international conflict resolution through the mechanisms of peacekeeping and peace-enforcement. But why is the reconstitution of political authority, in the event of a collapse, a necessary or desirable objective for the population concerned and/or the international system?

Politics as Authority

The major conflicts of the human race have been about authority, whether it be ecclesiastical, monarchical, or democratic.[9] The sources of laws, the obligations and responsibilities of rulers and subjects, and the division of responsibilities between competing organs of government are all fundamental questions of authority that have preoccupied political thinkers throughout history. Thus, for instance, Ibn Khaldun, a prominent Muslim scholar and jurist of the fourteenth century, noted that "authority is a noble and enjoyable position. It comprises all the good things of the world, the pleasures of the body, and the joys of the soul. Therefore, there is, as a rule, great competition for it."[10] David Easton, one of the preeminent political thinkers of the twentieth century, argues that politics is essentially the *authoritative* allocation of values. "An allocation is authoritative," he explains, "when the persons oriented to it consider that they are bound by it." [11]

The modern state is the product of an agreement on what constitutes authority structures in a given society. For the purpose of this chapter, how that consensus is reached, whether by the fiat of Hobbes's Leviathan or the democratic imperative of Rousseau's general will, is not nearly as important as the fact that an understanding exists on what constitutes authority in a given society. Essentially, therefore, authority comprises the social capacity for making and executing decisions; and the presence of a framework for the acceptance by the bulk of society of such decisions. According to Easton, these two critical variables "distinguish political systems from all other types of social systems. *Once events occur leaving it impossible for members of a system to arrive at political decisions, or, if after they have been taken, they are regularly rejected by large segments of the membership, no political system (democratic, totalitarian, or authoritarian) can function.* The system must either crumble into a variety of smaller units . . . or it must be absorbed into another society subject to a different political system."[12]

It follows logically, therefore, that the collapse of a political system is really about the collapse of authority. And its distinctive feature is the fragmentation of society into incoherent parts, each of which is unable to regulate its action and actors. Given this condition, not only will the probability of the outbreak of violent conflicts be higher, but such conflicts will be typically lacking in direction and organization. In such circumstances, the creation or recreation of authority becomes the mission of external interventionists, such as was implied by "peace-building" in *An Agenda for Peace*.[13] The failure of such intervention, therefore, to reconstitute authority in one form or another may then be viewed as a serious political and conceptual gaffe. Herein lies the fundamental problem of the current UN framework for conflict resolution.

Peace-Maintenance as a Teleological Imperative

The evolution of the concept and practice of UN peacekeeping in international politics is truly a remarkable story of institutional improvisation and ingenuity.[14] Indeed, as has been noted by Walter Clarke and Robert Gosende: "The UN Charter does not use the term peacekeeping; the word is defined by inference only in Chapters VI and VII."[15] One has only to look at the character of the global system of states in 1945 to see why the architects of the UN conceptualized global security along the strict lines of Chapter VI and Chapter VII. According to Michael Howard, "the founding fathers of the UN visualized an essentially static world system: one incrementally developing through peaceful change but in which 'peace and security' implied the maintenance of a status quo which only 'aggressors' (criminals whose motivation was irrelevant) would disturb."[16]

In such a world, changes *in* the system, which are, by definition, reformist in nature, will be determined by peaceful means. By contrast, the threat of systemic change, which is usually a challenge by an emerging power to reconstitute the global pecking order, must be met with the full force of the international community (by which is meant the great powers of the Security Council).[17] As long as this assumption mirrored the real world, then the security provisions of the UN Charter would suffice. The problem with this model, however, was that "in the world that was taking shape in the 1950s, the colonial structure of the late 1940s was the last thing that the majority of states wanted to preserve. For the newly created nations—and even more, those still aspiring to nationhood—the world was dynamic rather than static. Peace was to be sought not in the maintenance of order, but in the securing of justice. It was something to be achieved, if necessary fought for, rather than preserved."[18]

Confronted with this reality, the UN adapted its role in the area of international peace and security. According to Howard, it interpreted its role to be "the prevention of armed conflict and the peaceful resolution of disputes between *major powers*; and . . . the containment, failing reconciliation, of regional and civil conflicts, to prevent them from escalating to the point where they might affect global stability."[19] In practice, this meant that the UN had to tread carefully to avoid igniting or worsening great power rivalry. This had two consequences. First, the UN's method of conflict resolution necessarily relied on what Chopra refers to as a "diplomatic" framework. Accordingly, whenever it was absolutely necessary and politically feasible, "limited military forces and civilian personnel were deployed symbolically to guarantee negotiated settlements, invariably between two sovereign states" (but, in reality, between the great powers as well).[20] Clearly, this model considered prior consent to be a *sine qua non*. Not surprisingly, there were only fifteen such deployments between 1945 and 1989.[21] The second consequence of the UN's adaptation of its role in the security sphere was that it sacrificed the interests of smaller nations (which were usually the locus of insecurity) for those of the great powers. Nowhere was this more obvious than during the UN Operation in the Congo (ONUC)—an experience that "a generation of UN officials wanted to forget, or, if not forget, then never to repeat."[22]

The end of the Cold War in 1989 did not dramatically change the locus of conflict. Despite widespread violence in the Balkans and accompanying the dissolution of the Soviet Union, most conflicts continued to be fought in the developing parts of the world—the "Third World." However, the end of geostrategic competition did remove de facto security blankets that had covered some developing states, a change that reduced the likelihood of automatic involvement of the major powers in Third World conflicts. In these circumstances was born the UN's "second generation" of peace operations. "In the more challenging environment of internal conflicts, where the conventional necessity of consent of belligerent forces was not always forthcoming, the focus [of UN member states] shifted from mere diplomacy to the development of a limited and gradually intensifying use of armed force concept for multinational missions. . . . This period also witnessed the emergence of complex, multifunctional operations."[23]

While disparate uses of force were tested in Somalia and the former Yugoslavia, this was not preceded by nor did it result in a commonly agreed on doctrine. In both cases, Chopra adds, the missions also failed because they were initially conceived as *"diplomatic* peacekeeping" but deployed in *politically* "challenging environments."[24] This may be so, but the only way we can evaluate this argument is by defining the distinction between diplomacy and politics; and here we encounter the most fundamental weakness of the theory. According to Chopra:

> The UN tends to confuse the terms "diplomatic" and "political." It refers to the "political process" as the attempt to reach a degree of reconciliation between factions or states. This is considered "political" not just because the process addresses the conclusion of a long-term settlement between states, or the establishment of a unified executive authority internally, but also to distinguish it from the other dimensions of an operation—military security, humanitarian assistance, or electoral organization. . . . However, in such "political processes," the UN behaves as a diplomat and interlocutor, a representative of an authority far away, but fails to exercise political authority itself.[25]

If the problem with the existing framework is that the UN conflates "political processes" with "diplomatic processes" as Chopra contends, then his attempt to distinguish those processes has only compounded the matter. The UN *has to* act as an interlocutor when attempting to establish an *executive* machinery in a foreign land. Indeed, it has to act as an interlocutor, a diplomat, to be able to see through a resolution of the Security Council. Nor is the organization unique in its political-diplomatic role. The U.S. president is at once a foreign policy guru (a diplomat) and a *politician*, who must carry his constituency as well as successfully relate with congressional delegates with diverse interests and agendas. Essentially, therefore, the distinction between the political sphere and the diplomatic sphere becomes a questionable academic issue.

The question today is: Should the UN treat its peace operations as a political rather than diplomatic, economic, or military task? In my view, this question is the kernel of the much-discussed confusion surrounding the proposed reform of the organization and, even more specifically, its beleaguered administrative reforms.[26] The fact is that the UN, according to Jeane Kirkpatrick, is a "political system" concerned as much about ends as it is about *means*.[27] Consequently, rather than conceptualize the problem of UN peace operations as one of improper distinction between political and diplomatic processes and ends, my position is that the problem should be seen as the organization's penchant for compartmentalizing its operational responsibilities rather than evolving a holistic framework to deal with the multidimensional character of global peace and security.[28] Indeed, the strength of the theory of peace-maintenance rests in its recognition that, in practice, a political framework will entail the utilization of diverse means—judicial, administrative, economic, and moral instruments—to achieve set objectives.

In this regard, the theory argues that in the event of a deployment "the UN must establish a centre of gravity . . . around which local individuals and institutions can coalesce until a new authority structure is established and transferred to a local, legitimately determined leadership. . . . This implies that the UN claims jurisdiction over the entire territory, and ought to deploy throughout if it can. It establishes a direct relationship with the local population that will eventually participate in the reconstitution of authority, and which will inherit the newly established institutions."[29] Thus postulated, peace-maintenance is a blueprint for a government of the UN, by the UN, for an endangered population. It is, therefore, the last stage of the teleological evolution of the UN as the central player in the human quest for world order.[30] Peace-maintenance, then, becomes the quintessential art of politics defined as authority. It is "an overall blue umbrella, under which law and order are maintained"; it is "all-pervasive and is connected to the total social process locally"; and it is "an outside guarantor of a kind of internal self-determination."[31]

This definition raises two interrelated questions. First, is the UN capable of assuming direct executive tasks in collapsed states? The answer: obviously not. As Kofi Annan conceded when he was under-secretary-general for peacekeeping operations, "the political *cum* financial crisis" arising from current operations has led to a view within the Secretariat and the major capitals of the world "that the Organization should do less peace-keeping, either by not getting involved at all in certain conflicts or by working only at their *margins*."[32] The organization has so far responded to these circumstances by downscaling existing missions or contracting out to regional organizations those missions that must contend with "hot button" issues (such as in the former Yugoslavia); and in many other conflicts (such as Rwanda), it has either hesitated to get involved or has resisted outright.[33] Because of the organization's financial and institutional constraints, in other words, "triage" is already a key policy component when the UN considers intervention.[34]

The current financial and administrative weaknesses of the UN need not dampen the world's optimism for a positively proactive UN. Indeed, as we have already seen, it has stimulated new thinking, such as the idea of peace-maintenance under consideration in this volume. And as Annan has argued, "in our present world and into the foreseeable future, there is no such thing as international non-involvement in violent conflicts."[35] It is against this background that we should pose the second question. Under what circumstances would the population of collapsed states accept the authority of the UN?

Accepting the Authority of the UN

Historians and activists who remember the League of Nations "mandate" and UN "trusteeship" systems (which turned Namibia and Somalia, for instance, into new colonies) find the explicit political realism of the theory of peace-maintenance to be morally disturbing. This is because proponents of peace-maintenance are driven fundamentally by the all-too-familiar and recent specter of savagery occasioned by "warlordism" in parts of Africa and central Europe. [36] In the current environment of despair, in which it has become intellectually and politically fashionable to speak of recolonization as a humanitarian act,[37] the theory of peace-maintenance creditably confronts the dilemma based on rational-actor assumptions. For the UN, such an assumption of executive capacity in troubled spots would untie the organization's hand, thereby unleashing its full managerial ingenuity. Obviously, for the masses of the troubled population, both the liberation from insecurity and improved prospects for better life should offset the limitation of sovereignty, which is after all only a temporary phenomenon. This arrangement also has the added advantage of being a *covenant* and, even more important, a covenant that is openly arrived at. The element of choice here derives from the understanding that if a society does not want a "UN government," it had better not become a bleeding sore in the anatomy of international life. This path of inquiry encourages us to return to political theory for guidance.

To facilitate our understanding of the conditions under which any population would accept an authority structure, it would be useful to step back somewhat and pose the question: What are the implications or effects of authority on a population? The effect of every political authority is to reward and/or punish individuals. Political authority is, therefore, Janus-faced. It may facilitate or enhance individual reproduction, security, and the attainment of the general good; but it may also hinder the pursuit of such values. According to Easton, "an [authoritative] allocation may *deprive* a person of a valued thing already possessed; it may *obstruct* the attainment of values which would otherwise have been obtained; or it may give some persons access to values and *deny* them to others."[38]

Because of a general appreciation of the significant effect it can have on human lives, individuals are concerned about authority. Similarly, political structures are not complacent. The consequence of these dynamics is that society is constantly subjected to individual adjustments to either of the two faces of authority. This leads us to an analysis of four important variables that influence the acceptance of UN authority by any given population: self-interest; the responsible use of coercion; the legitimacy of authority; and tradition or socialization. [39]

Self-Interest:
Meeting the Socioeconomic Needs of Individuals

Individuals respond to authority on the basis of self-interest. These interests may vary, but chief among them are security and economic improvement. That individuals consciously or unconsciously make sociopolitical and economic decisions based on varying calculations of their interests is the basis of rational choice theory. One of the major failings of comparative analyses in the past few decades has been the tendency to exclude from this generalization some human populations, simply on the basis of their position in the global hierarchy of states as "developed" or "developing." Thus, for instance, only by assuming a diminution of the capacity of populations in failed states to make rational decisions could the UN fail to foresee the problems that arose with the "technicals" in Somalia.[40] In this particular case, the planners of UNOSOM II had erroneously hypothesized that individuals in conditions of anarchy are likely to be unable to make decisions rationally. Planners anticipated an attitude of "anything goes." The reality is that individuals in the highly stressful conditions of collapsed states are more likely to think rationally because their decisions are simply about life and death. The young Somali would, not surprisingly, escort a UN or humanitarian convoy as well as a gang of looters in exchange for cash or commodity to enable him to reproduce himself and his family. In such circumstances, authority has no name, no face, no creed, nor color; it is merely a function of rationality.

What this means is that a UN authority must be functionally relevant. To do so, it must strive to meet the material and social needs of the population under its control. This is the very essence of the "social contract," the violation of which led to the collapse of the previous political system and hence to the intervention of the UN. Obviously, the issues here are institutional responsibility and accountability. As one student of UN peace operations recently emphasized, "the UN cannot remain aloof from its relationship to territory and local population, over which it may have claimed jurisdiction, and therefore must recognize its role in the exercise of executive political authority."[41]

There is some evidence that the UN is beginning to think seriously about these issues, at least conceptually. The idea of "positive inducements," which has been broached in the organization, is aimed at addressing the current gap between the physical presence of the UN in troubled countries and its reluctance to assume concomitant responsibility in the socioeconomic realm. According to Annan, the UN may provide a "structure of rewards" in a mission area through "any variety of activities." Incentives might include "development assistance of various types, local infrastructure and water projects, the provision of access to small business loans, making available (or, better yet, training people to provide) basic medical care and veterinary services. To employ them effectively as tools of conflict resolution requires understanding people's problems in their complexity and being able to respond at several levels simultaneously and with a certain amount of flexibility." Annan warns, however, that *"in UN operations as currently constituted, there is neither structure, staff, nor budget for this type of activity."*[42] Is it any surprise, then, that populations have generally tended to respond negatively toward a UN presence, leading ultimately to the high incidence of mission failure? The point is that populations will be more likely to accept UN authority if they see that the new dispensation offers them improved security and better access to economic opportunities, conditions described by Richard Cousens and Antonio Donini in their chapters. Conversely, when the UN's performance in these areas approximates the dismal record of the previous regime, then a local community will more likely be disposed to question and challenge the authority of the UN.

Responsible Use of Coercion

The functional relevance of UN missions is only one aspect of the equation. The executive capability which is required by peace-maintenance also necessitates the development of a credible coercive capability. Law enforcement is an executive task par excellence, and it cannot be fulfilled without visible and credible coercion. That political systems require this capability in order to function has long been recognized by political theorists, as illustrated in Mark Plunkett's "justice packages." Easton observes that populations may accept "allocations [of values] as binding on the grounds of fear of the use of force" or other sanctions.[43] To be effective, a political system must have the ability to reward populations, hence its social and economic functions. But it must also be able to punish those who disobey the law. The coercive instrument of a political system is therefore designed to punish as well as *deter* offenders.

Until now, the transformation of UN peace operations has hinged on the quantitative and qualitative aspects of a multinational coercive presence.[44] Previously, classical or first-generation peacekeeping involved in its areas of operation a small and barely visible coercive presence. In these kinds of missions, it was normal to deploy in a conflict zone unarmed military observers, numbering only in the low hundreds. Even where deployments of a few thousand were lightly armed, they were under strict instructions not to use force unless in unequivocal situations of self-defense. Typically, their numbers and capability made them insignificant factors in the conflict resolution equation. How does a population numbering in millions take notice of several hundred unarmed personnel spread thinly over thousands of kilometers?

Not surprisingly, the resolution or continuation of the conflicts for which first-generation peacekeepers—such as the UN Emergency Force (UNEF) in the Sinai between 1956 and 1967—were deployed tended to occur *in spite* of the presence of these UN forces. As Gen. Bruno Loi, commander of the Italian contingent in Somalia, once remarked about UNOSOM I peacekeeping: "It remains a mystery how the UN thought it could use 500 troops to contain violence, protect a civilian population and ensure the safe delivery of humanitarian aid throughout Somalia, a country the size of Italy, Spain and Portugal put together."[45] Ironically, however, even the significant increase in firepower which defined many post-Cold War peace-enforcement operations, such as in UNOSOM II and parts of UNPRO-FOR, also failed to make a decisive impact on the conflict situations. This is due as much to the lopsided focus on coercion relative to "positive inducements," as it is to the glaring disjuncture between a minimal enforcement capability and the extensive range of mission tasks that require robust coercion.[46]

Matching force to need is important, but even more important in the particular circumstances of peace operations is ensuring that coercion is employed responsibly and impartially. Efforts must be made to avoid repeating the previous status quo. In situations where anarchy has resulted from the abuse of power by the collapsed authority, nothing would better guarantee the revulsion of a population than a repeated pattern of abuse of power by UN forces. In Somalia, for instance, the acrimony that ensued because of the irresponsible use of force by elements of the Belgian and Canadian contingents, as well as at times U.S. forces, paralleled a chain of events that led ultimately to the failure of UNOSOM II.[47] At issue was the disagreement among Somalis to replace the indigenous despotism (that is, abuse of authority) by Mohammed Siyad Barre with another, either domestic or foreign, amorphous and potentially deadlier. The historical lesson of the past century or so of human evolution is that arbitrary exercise of power turns an otherwise placid population against authority.[48]

Legitimacy of Authority

To argue that political *authority* has to be *legitimate* to ensure its acceptability to local populations comes precariously close to pleonasm: strictly speaking, authority is a function of legitimacy, as Andy Knight and Sally Morphet have illustrated. Yet we need to make the emphasis because, all too often, regimes have been accorded international recognition and legitimacy by, among all other actors, the UN. The extent to which the UN has accorded de facto legitimacy to unconstitutional regimes in Africa and much of the developing world has yet to be seriously examined by the scholarly community. Authority is the product of a contract, albeit one that is not always visible, between rulers and hoi polloi. As I stated earlier, many of the struggles leading to the collapse of states have been about controversies that center on the illegitimacy of regimes. Not surprisingly, as Zartman's study shows, some of the more successful instances of reversing state collapse have taken the form of "democratic transitions"—that is, an attempt, even if ridden with faults, to seek a popular basis of support for government.[49]

Nothing could be more damaging to the prestige and substance of the UN than even the mere perception among any population that the organization is engaged in new forms of colonialism. Such a charge has often been leveled against some powerful states and international organizations whose actions in developing countries displayed an insensitivity to glaring power disequilibrium. For this reason, it is insufficient to argue, as Chopra does, that UN authority as envisaged by the theory of peace-maintenance is *not* colonialism merely because "colonial domination is a unilateral enterprise" drawing "resources from a colony," while a UN-centered administration is "a joint interim authority" that is collectively accountable.[50] That distinction will remain within the sphere of theory if the purveyors of UN authority fail to "respond to local needs with *political, anthropological and sociological sensitivity.*"[51] What guarantees are there, really, that the UN authority will not imitate the colonialism of European states in the mid-nineteenth century and the indigenous despotism that led to the collapse of new states at the end of the twentieth century? Such guarantees are beyond the realm of the theory of peace-maintenance or any theory for that matter. They are, instead, the property of human beings as actors and social operators. Unfortunately, there is enough in recent human history to encourage skepticism about the practice of peace-maintenance.

Tradition or Socialization

Closely related to legitimacy is the factor of tradition or socialization as a determinant of the acceptability of UN authority. Human beings are an embodiment of history and experience. Indeed, an average individual is a walking library and art museum. Our behavior is influenced by what we learn and how we learn it, as well as by our experiences and the timing of those experiences. Socialization—that is, the transmission of values from one generation of humans to another—is essentially a reproductive exercise on a societal scale. Much of the socialization in the world today occurs at the level of the nation-state, thereby assuring its reproduction. The concept of the "nation-state" itself conveys both authority and territoriality. In this sense, it draws our attention to the proximity of authority to territory, and hence to the territorial character of socialization. Very few human populations, if any, are socialized to accept a distant authority. The objective of nationalism is to assure that this does not happen. Therefore, a UN authority must seriously embark on social engineering on a scale large enough and deep enough to ensure its acceptance by successive generations of a given population. The enormity of such a task is too obvious to warrant any elaboration in this essay.

Conclusion:
Bringing People Back into the Peace Equation

The essence of peace-maintenance is to bring people back as rapidly as possible into any enduring framework for conflict resolution. For too long, however, people have been neglected in the peace calculus by the UN and its state-sponsors. Analyzing U.S. participation in peace operations, for example, Clarke and Gosende accurately observe that "the debate over any US intervention usually revolves around the amount of time the military component will be deployed. The duration of the operation is usually driven by the calendar rather than by measures of effectiveness" or improved human conditions. *"Although the plight of the local population will have been the stimulus to the original operation, the victims tend to be forgotten in the subsequent arguments over tasks appropriate to the military component of the operation."* Clarke and Gosende conclude that "no US mission should be so narrowly defined that its concerns for force protection hamper its ability to support those engaged in humanitarian activities."[52]

One of the most serious flaws of politics in this century is the extraordinary amount of intellectual and material resources devoted to states rather than people. The theory of peace-maintenance departs significantly from this trend and focuses on people rather than states. It is therefore a serious intellectual effort to return the UN to the preamble of its Charter: "We the peoples of the United Nations. . . ." In this regard, the theory assumes (quite accurately) that "the world [has] become interdependent and sovereignty [is] no longer absolute or exclusive."[53]

The dilemma of world politics, however, is that, despite the increasing interdependence of peoples of all races and nationalities, power remains in the hands of governments or transnational actors who still regard their states of origin as their final sanctuaries.[54] As I have argued in this chapter, national identification persists because of a combination of concrete objective factors, such as security and material reproduction, which the state assures; and subjective or sentimental factors, which are the product of socialization.

To be accepted by the population in a collapsed state, where the security and material reproductive functions of the state are no longer fulfilled, a UN intervention would do well to fill this gap. Indeed, in political peace-maintenance, legitimacy will depend on effectiveness, and eventual effectiveness will be determined by legitimacy. The sentimental factors that influence people's acceptance of authority are much deeper, and take a considerable time to change. But when people realize the positive effects of new authority structures on their lives, they tend to respond favorably to those structures. The success of liberal democracy in Germany and Japan owes a great deal to the genius of American statesmanship in these countries after World War II. In my view, the postwar period of Allied (U.S.) occupation of Germany and Japan (and, we may add, the subsequent occupation of South Korea) is the model of peace-maintenance that the UN is searching for. It is worth noting, in that case, that it took both the authority of a General MacArthur and the vision of a George Marshall to pull off these successes.[55] ⊕

Notes

Clement E. Adibe is an assistant professor of political science at DePaul University in Chicago. He was formerly a Killam postdoctoral fellow at Dalhousie University and published *Managing Arms in Peace Processes: Somalia* with the United Nations Institute for Disarmament Research (UNIDIR).

1. Compare Jarat Chopra, "The space of peace-maintenance," *Political Geography* 15, no. 3/4 (March–April 1996): 335–357; William Pfaff, "A New Colonialism? Europe Must Go Back to Africa," *Foreign Affairs* 74, no. 1 (January–February 1995): 2–6; Ali A. Mazrui, "Decaying Parts of Africa Need Benign Colonization," *International Herald Tribune*, 4 August 1994, p. 6; Mazrui, "Pan-Africanism: From Poetry to Power," *Issue* 23, no. 1 (winter–spring 1995): 35–38.

2. See Kofi A. Annan, "Peace Operations and the United Nations: Preparing for the Next Century," New York, UN Department of Peace Keeping Operations, manuscript, 1996; Thomas G. Weiss, ed., "Beyond UN Subcontracting: Task-Sharing with Regional Security Arrangements and Service-Providing NGOs," *Third World Quarterly* 18, no. 3 (special issue, 1997).

3. See John Mackinlay and Jarat Chopra, "Second Generation Multinational Operations," *The Washington Quarterly* 15, no. 3 (summer 1992): 113–131; John Mackinlay, "Powerful Peacekeepers," *Survival.* 32, no. 3 (May–June 1990): 241–250; Chopra, "The space of peace-maintenance," p. 337.

4. Compare Boutros Boutros-Ghali, *An Agenda for Peace: Preventive Diplomacy, Peacemaking and Peace-keeping* (New York: United Nations Department of Public Information, 1992); William J. Durch, ed., *The Evolution of UN Peacekeeping: Case Studies and Comparative Analysis* (New York: St. Martin's Press, 1993); I. William Zartman, ed., *Collapsed States: The Disintegration and Restoration of Legitimate Authority* (Boulder: Lynne Rienner, 1995); and Chopra, "The space of peace-maintenance," pp. 335–337.

5. Chopra, "The space of peace-maintenance," p. 336.

6. I. William Zartman, "Introduction: Posing the Problem of State Collapse," in Zartman, *Collapsed States*, pp. 1–11.

7. Ibid., p. 1 (italics added).

8. Ibid., p. 5.

9. Indeed, the classic works of Thucydides, *History of the Peloponnesian War* (circa 400 B.C.), and of Thomas Hobbes, *The Leviathan* (1650), which have influenced generations of thought in international politics, were studies of conflicts about the locus of authority in Greece and England, respectively. Similarly, the American civil war, the Russian revolutionary war, and the nationalist wars of Europe that produced the modern nation-state in the first place were essentially conflicts about authority. See Charles Tilly, ed., *The Formation of the National State in Western Europe* (Princeton: Princeton University Press, 1975), especially chap. 1–2, 4; Bernard Semmel, ed. *Marxism and the Science of War* (New York: Oxford University Press, 1981).

10. Ibn Khaldun, "Four Kinds of War," in Lawrence Freedman, ed., *War* (Oxford University Press, 1994), pp. 89–90.

11. David Easton, *A Framework for Political Analysis* (Englewood Cliffs, N.J.: Prentice-Hall, 1965), p. 50.

12. Ibid., p. 96 (italics added).

13. See Boutros-Ghali, *An Agenda for Peace*, part VI.

14. For useful discussions and analyses, see: William J. Durch, "Introduction," in Durch, *The Evolution of UN Peacekeeping*, pp. 1–4; Michael Howard,

"The Historical Development of the UN's Role in International Security," in Adam Roberts and Benedict Kingsbury, eds., *United Nations, Divided World*, 2d ed. (Oxford: Clarendon Press, 1993), pp. 63–80; Thomas G. Weiss and Jarat Chopra, *United Nations Peacekeeping: An ACUNS Teaching Text* (Hanover, N.H.: Academic Council on the United Nations System, 1992).

15. Walter Clarke and Robert Gosende, "The Political Component: The Missing Vital Element in US Intervention Planning," *Parameters* 26, no. 3 (autumn 1996): 42. See also Christopher Brady and Sam Daws, "UN Operations: The Political-Military Interface," *International Peacekeeping* 1, no. 1 (spring 1994): 64–65.

16. Howard, "The Historical Development of the UN's Role in International Security," p. 68.

17. For further discussions of systemic challenges, see Robert Gilpin, *War and Change in World Politics* (Cambridge: Cambridge University Press, 1981).

18. Howard, "The Historical Development of the UN's Role in International Security," pp. 68–69.

19. Ibid., p. 69 (italics added).

20. Chopra, "The space of peace-maintenance," p. 337.

21. For a detailed survey of the operations during this period, see Alan James, *Peacekeeping in International Politics* (London: Macmillan Press, 1990); compare 2d ed. and 3d ed. of UN, *The Blue Helmets: A Review of United Nations Peacekeeping* (New York: United Nations Department of Public Information, 1990, 1996).

22. William J. Durch, "The UN Operation in the Congo: 1960–1964," in Durch, *The Evolution of UN Peacekeeping*, p. 316.

23. Chopra, "The space of peace-maintenance," p. 337.

24. Ibid., p. 338.

25. Ibid.

26. See Thomas G. Weiss, David P. Forsythe, and Roger A. Coate, *The United Nations and Changing World Politics* (Boulder: Westview, 1997), especially chap. 4; Antonio Donini, "The Bureaucracy and Free Spirits: Stagnation and Innovation in the Relationship Between the UN and NGOs," in Thomas G. Weiss and Leon Gordenker, eds., *NGOs, the UN and Global Governance* (Boulder: Lynne Rienner, 1996), pp. 83–101; Brian Urquhart and Erskine Childers, "Towards a More Effective United Nations," *Development Dialogue* 1–2 (1991): 1–96. See most recently Secretary-General Kofi Annan's proposals in "Renewing the United Nations: Programme for Reform," UN Doc. A/51/1950 of 16 July 1997.

27. Jeane Kirkpatrick, "The United Nations as a Political System: A Practicing Political Scientist's Insights into U.N. Politics," *World Affairs* 146, no. 4 (spring 1984): 358–364.

28. As I see it, this was the lost message of Boutros-Ghali's manifesto in *An Agenda for Peace*. He tried, perhaps belatedly, to restate it in his *Agenda for Development*. For details, see his *Building Peace and Development* (New York: United Nations Department of Public Information, 1994); Clarke and Gosende, "The Political Component," especially pp. 40–49; critically compare the three parts on international peace and security, human rights and humanitarian affairs, and building peace through sustainable development in Weiss et al., *The United Nations and Changing World Politics*.

29. Chopra, "The space of peace-maintenance," p. 339.

30. Chopra argues elsewhere that peace-maintenance is indeed "the last stage of development." See Jarat Chopra, "Peace-Maintenance: The Last Stage of Development," *Global Society* 11, no. 2 (May 1997): 185–204.

31. Chopra, "The space of peace-maintenance," p. 339.

32. Annan, "Peace Operations and the United Nations," p. 1 (italics added).

33. See Thomas G. Weiss, "The End of Appeasement in Bosnia?" *Providence Journal Bulletin*, 12 March 1994, p. A12; Peter Hammond, *Holocaust in Rwanda* (Capetown, South Africa: Frontline Fellowship, 1996); *Issue: A Journal of Opinion* 23, no. 2 (special volume, summer 1995).

34. See Annan, "Peace Operations and the United Nations," especially pp. 14–27; Thomas Weiss, "Triage: Humanitarian Interventions in a New Era," *World Policy Journal* 11, no. 1 (spring 1994): 59–68; Edward Marks and William Lewis, eds., *Triage for Failing States*, McNair Paper, no. 26, (Washington, D.C.: National Defense University, January 1994).

35. Annan, "Peace Operations and the United Nations," p. 2.

36. For a penetratingly critical analysis of African and Central European case studies, see Julius O. Ihonvbere, "Beyond Warlords and Clans: The African Crisis and the Somali Situation," *International Third World Studies Journal and Review* 6 (1994): 7–19; David Binder, "Anatomy of a Massacre," *Foreign Policy*, no. 97 (winter 1994/95): 70–78.

37. This is the thrust of the arguments in Pfaff, "A New Colonialism," and Mazrui, "Decaying Parts of Africa Need Benign Colonization." For a critique of this position, see Timothy M. Shaw and Clement E. Adibe, "Africa and Global Developments in the Twenty-First Century," *International Journal* 51, no. 1 (winter 1995/96): 1–26.

38. Easton, *A Framework for Political Analysis*, p. 50 (italics added).

39. Ibid., p. 50.

40. For further details, see Clement E. Adibe, *Managing Arms in Peace Processes: Somalia* (Geneva: UNIDIR, 1995), chap. 4; F.M. Lorenz, "Law and Anarchy in Somalia," *Parameters* 23, no. 4 (winter 1993/94), especially p. 40, note 3.

41. Chopra, "The space of peace-maintenance," p. 339.

42. Annan, "Peace Operations and the United Nations," p. 12 (italics added).

43. Easton, *A Framework for Political Analysis*, p. 50.

44. Compare Mackinlay and Chopra, "Second Generation Multinational Operations," pp. 113–131; Brian Urquhart, "Beyond the 'Sheriff's Posse'," *Survival* 32, no. 3 (May–June 1990): 196–205; Chopra, "The space of peace-maintenance," especially pp. 337–357.

45. Gen. Bruno Loi, interview by author. Geneva, Switzerland, 29 March 1995.

46. Lorenz, "Law and Anarchy in Somalia," pp. 27–41.

47. Significantly enough, the Canadian government dissolved the Airborne Regiment that produced the "rogue" soldiers, and conducted a large-scale public judicial inquiry into the training and military doctrine of the armed forces, and into a high-level cover-up: see the five-volume report of the Commission of Inquiry into the Deployment of Canadian Forces to Somalia, *Dishonoured Legacy: The Lessons of the Somalia Affair* (Ottawa: Public Works and Government Services Canada, 1997).

48. For in-depth historical and comparative analysis, see Barrington Moore, *Social Origins of Dictatorship and Democracy: Lord and Peasant in the Making of the Modern World* (Boston: Beacon Press, 1966).

49. See especially Donald Rothchild, "Rawlings and the Engineering of Legitimacy in Ghana," in Zartman, *Collapsed States*, chap. 4; I. William Zartman, "Putting Things Back Together," in Zartman, *Collapsed States*, chap. 17. John Stremlau would argue quite strongly that "opening political space" is an "antidote to anarchy." See John Stremlau, "Antidote to Anarchy," *The Washington Quarterly* 18, no. 1 (winter 1995): 29–44.

50. Chopra, "The space of peace-maintenance," pp. 340–341.

51. Ibid., p. 341 (italics added).

52. Clarke and Gosende, "The Political Component," pp. 43–44 (italics added).

53. Chopra, "The space of peace-maintenance," p. 342. For further details, see Jarat Chopra and Thomas G. Weiss, "Sovereignty is no Longer Sacrosanct: Codifying Humanitarian Intervention," *Ethics and International Affairs* 6 (1992): 95–117.

54. Compare Robert Keohane and Joseph S. Nye, Jr., eds., *Transnational Relations and World Politics* (Cambridge: Harvard University Press, 1972); Raymond Vernon, *Sovereignty at Bay: The Multinational Spread of U.S. Enterprises* (New York: Basic Books, 1971); and Keohane and Nye, *Power and Interdependence: World Politics in Transition* (Boston: Little, Brown, 1977); Keohane, *After Hegemony* (Princeton, N.J.: Princeton University Press, 1984).

55. See Thomas G. Weiss, "Intervention: Whither the United Nations?" *The Washington Quarterly* 17, no. 1 (winter 1994): especially 119–124.

8

Critiquing Peace-Maintenance

⊕

Duane Bratt

P eace-maintenance is an innovative concept designed to alleviate the problem of fractured societies through a harmonization of diplomatic, humanitarian, civilian, and military objectives as part of an overall political framework. However, unlike other concepts in the peace operations lexicon—such as peacekeeping, peacemaking, peace-enforcement, and peace-building—peace-maintenance has yet to undergo a rigorous debate over its merits and deficiencies.[1] Now that this edited volume has fleshed out peace-maintenance beyond Jarat Chopra's initial proposal,[2] it is time for the holes in the concept, some of them gaping, to be identified.

The purpose of this final chapter is to critique the arguments for and against peace-maintenance. My intention is not to bury peace-maintenance but to spur on its development by asking the hard questions. The analysis that follows is divided into three sections. The first, the politics of peace-maintenance, assesses the need for organizing civil administration and reestablishing law and order. The second section, the military and peace-maintenance, examines calls for providing military security, creating a UN army, and guaranteeing military impartiality. And the third section, the challenges in peace-maintenance, considers subcontracting complex tasks, asserting humanitarianism, accepting external authority, and financing joint operations.

The Politics of Peace-Maintenance

The authors of this book do a commendable job of showing that there is an urgent need for political peace-maintenance. They are also quite cognizant of the substantial obstacles facing the peace-maintenance concept. Andy Knight, in particular, highlights four problems: (1) the local population may view external authority as neoimperialism or neocolonialism; (2) civil wars are very complicated affairs with multiple root causes; (3) the rump existence of a state government will lead to issues of sovereignty; and (4) peace-maintenance may be seen to target only small, poor, and underdeveloped states. Unfortunately, like the other authors, Knight fails to identify or develop a procedure for how peace-maintenance could over-come these hurdles. This is a significant deficiency. Until peace-mainte-nance doctrine can be articulated sufficiently to account for such barriers facing its implementation, it will never become operational.

Organizing Civil Administration

Sally Morphet describes the UN's weaknesses in civil administration dur-ing its second-generation deployments in Namibia, Western Sahara, Cam-bodia, Angola, Mozambique, and El Salvador. She finds that the UN has been generally more successful in the electoral exercises of people's civil administration than in governmental civil administration. Given this con-clusion, why does the UN not restrict itself to supervising or conducting elections? How can the UN effectively assume executive tasks of admin-istration? Morphet suggests improved planning, increased resources, and a stronger political commitment from member states. While these are ad-mirable recommendations, they have all been made before and have had little impact on changing the fundamentally uncoordinated nature of UN peace operations.[3]

Morphet also recognizes that peace-maintenance operations work best when they have moral authority, appropriate organization, and an ability to provide information, and when they are impartial and supported by the local community. How many past operations have met this standard? How many future operations will be able to do so? Does she mean that conflicts where such conditions are impossible will be excluded from the peace-maintenance treatment? There would be a high moral price to pay for ig-noring tough, usually humanitarian, operations. Are innocent civilians to die because the UN will not protect humanitarian shipments? Is the interna-tional community prepared to accept the destruction and loss of life caused by seemingly intractable conflicts? Are civilians in conflicts where Mor-phet's standard cannot be met worth less than those in calmer environments?

Reestablishing Law and Order

Mark Plunkett persuasively argues that reestablishing law and order is a prerequisite for peace-maintenance. Peace without justice, he says, is likely to result in a breach birth for a new nation. This point was starkly il-lustrated in July 1997 when Cambodia's co–prime minister, Hun Sen, launched a successful coup virtually negating the $2–3 billion election conducted by the United Nations Transitional Authority in Cambodia (UNTAC). Plunkett's formula for reestablishing law and order rests on in-cluding in operations a justice package, which mixes a standardized prac-tical manual (based on the experience of past missions) with specific pro-tocols developed for each particular crisis as it arises. Plunkett enumerates the many requirements of a justice package: a UN criminal law and procedure; a panel of distinguished international jurists; UN special prosecutions; specialized resources; commissions of inquiry; a survey and assessment of existing justice assets; the selection of acceptable local personnel; judicial training; police training; the independence of civilian police (CIVPOL) officers; the training of prosecutors and defenders; detention centers and alternatives to imprisonment; physical security for justice personnel; anticorruption measures; and adequate legal resources.

There are several flaws in Plunkett's approach. First, the inclusion in peace-maintenance of a justice package with coercive sanctions may prolong the fighting. The tribunals at Nuremberg and Tokyo demonstrated that the losing side in a conflict is more likely to be prosecuted. Therefore, as Timothy Mak has remarked, "If all sides know that if they win they will simply be able to refuse to hand their own soldiers over, and if they lose they will be (happily) handed over to the Tribunal by the victorious enemy, what incentive is there to 'surrender'? The only incentive is to win (and keep killing)."[4]

Second, how will the UN be able to ensure that political witch-hunts and show trials do not occur? When peace finally comes to a country, civilians will demand justice, but some may use the opportunity to exact revenge upon their political or personal enemies. How will the UN prevent vendettas—like those that have occurred in Germany, where former East Germans have been digging into Stassi records to determine which of their neighbors were spies or collaborators? This issue would be greatly exacerbated if the UN dared to adopt capital punishment and execute convicted war criminals. Currently, the UN is under pressure to reverse its effective abolition of the death penalty. For example, members of the Tutsi-dominated Rwandan government have demanded that Hutus who ordered the genocide be executed. Victims may feel that, without recourse to capital punishment, the UN is imposing on a state lenient forms of punishment that stop justice from being served. It may prove difficult for the UN to justify excluding capital punishment when a number of member states, particularly the United States, retain it to enforce their own penal codes. However, a UN reversal of its position on capital punishment would raise a whole new set of problems for the reestablishment of law and order in war-torn states.

Third, much of the discussion on war crimes tribunals is based on an erroneous analogy with the Nuremberg trials at the end of World War II. Nuremberg had four unique features: hostilities had ended; the losing side was completely defeated; the victorious powers were willing to prosecute individuals suspected of committing war crimes, while observing due process; and such individuals were physically within the territory of a victor or defeated nation, or a friendly third country, and could therefore be apprehended by the Allied occupying forces.[5] Were comparable conditions present in the former Yugoslavia, Rwanda, Cambodia, Somalia, or Haiti? Will they likely exist in any future civil war?

Fourth, many from senior echelons—those most responsible for the atrocities committed during the conflict—may be able to bargain their way out of prosecution.[6] This happened in Haiti where the leaders of the military junta (Lt. Gen. Raoul Cédras and Brig. Gen. Philippe Biamby) obtained amnesty from prosecution as part of the 1994 peace accords. Amnesties will continue to be given because the imperatives of peace will contradict the need for justice (or revenge) through criminal prosecution. This order of priority is sure to undermine any effort to establish an impartial rule of law. Resentment will come from many corners. Civilians will wonder why the UN let the worst offenders escape, and defendants will curse the fact that their lack of bargaining power, rather than any conception of justice, is why they alone are facing prosecution. In short, the necessity of amnesty to achieve peace will erode the legitimacy of any justice package.

The Military and Peace-Maintenance

Providing Military Security

In his chapter on providing military security, Richard Cousens is adamant that "muddling through" is not an option. This point cannot be disputed. Unfortunately, muddling through will continue to be the UN's signature. Until a permanent UN army is established—which is unlikely—any military force formed under the auspices of the UN will continue to be ad hoc. Thus, rapid deployment, command and control, logistical support, training and equipment, and communication will continue to be debilitating problems.[7]

A certain hypocrisy characterizes the views of those UN member states that possess the most powerful militaries. The five permanent members of the Security Council (P-5) are the fiercest critics of the UN's military capability, but they are also the staunchest opponents of providing the world organization with an expanded or independent military component. Any proposal for restructuring the UN's military capacity must account for this contradiction.

Cousens also argues that politicization of command posts dangerously threatens a mission's successful outcome. Again, it is difficult to argue this point on military grounds. However, the UN–as a *universal* international organization–is, and must be, committed to the principle of geographic representation, albeit within reason.[8] Since most conflicts occur in the developing world, it is only natural that peace operations include third world armies. However, a military force composed of privates from

Southern countries but generals from Western nations is not the answer. Such a force would lack political legitimacy in both the targeted state and the General Assembly and would greatly hinder the objectives of peace-maintenance. The connotations of Pakistani or Jordanian soldiers serving American or British officers in some failed state would resemble European armies in Asia and Africa prior to independence and would reek of neo-colonialism. In short, the security arm of peace-maintenance must reconcile the dilemma between military effectiveness and political legitimacy.

Creating a UN Army

According to Knight, an ideal requirement for establishing political authority in peace-maintenance should eventually be the creation of permanent UN police and military forces. In recent years, prominent individuals like Brian Urquhart[9] and member states like Canada[10] have proposed variations on the idea of a UN army. As with peace-maintenance itself, UN standing forces would face substantial obstacles. Adam Roberts succinctly summarizes the counterarguments:

- The responsibilities of an army would be too numerous and complex for the UN to realistically handle.
- The likely locale in civil wars and failed states presents unique problems for a UN army. Responses to internal conflicts must be long-term commitments and require a heavy administrative role. Moreover, such crises may not genuinely constitute threats to international security.
- The early injection of a military force into a conflict may not necessarily avert tragedy.
- If a UN army was designed to be a pathfinder for a subsequent, and traditional, peacekeeping force, it may have withdrawn before its services were most urgently needed.
- The use of force in humanitarian operations remains controversial.
- The existence of a UN army may encourage the Security Council to intervene more frequently.
- There remain doubts about the suitability of the Security Council as a military decisionmaking body.
- Member states may resist endowing the UN with an independent military capacity.
- A small quick reaction force may underestimate the size of forces required for certain urgent tasks.
- A UN army might not be more prepared to sustain casualties than national contingents.
- A UN army would require significant financing, which does not seem to be forthcoming for much less.

- A UN army would weaken efforts to include regional bodies in international peace and security.
- There are risks in the UN being seen primarily as a military organization.[11]

These hurdles have managed to block, and will likely continue to block, the establishment of a UN army. Therefore, if peace-maintenance is to evolve further, it cannot depend on the creation of permanent forces for its implementation.

Guaranteeing Military Impartiality

In peace-maintenance doctrine, military force is not strictly to be used impartially between the parties to the conflict, but rather impartially in enforcing Security Council mandates. In his introduction, Jarat Chopra asserts that impartiality should be defined as the objectivity with which a mandate is executed rather than the degree of the UN's submission to the will of the parties in conflict. However, this is a flawed interpretation of impartiality. The purpose of impartiality is to show that the UN is an "honest broker," with no interests other than to assist the warring parties achieve a peaceful resolution of their conflict. Once the UN takes sides, its role as an honest broker breaks down and any initiative it takes becomes suspect. There may be times when the troops can enforce their mandate without prejudice. For example, UN soldiers can use force against non–parties to the conflict, like criminals or rogue battalions, when they violate the mandate. Likewise, a UN force can take action in isolated circumstances against one of the parties. However, if a belligerent makes the conscious decision to violate part, or all, of the international mandate, then peacekeepers cannot force them to adhere.

The ramifications of not being impartial *between* the parties can be seen in Bosnia, where the UN and the North Atlantic Treaty Organization (NATO) were clearly biased against the Bosnian Serbs. According to a 1995 Secretary-General's report, "In all cases air power was used against Bosnian Serb targets or targets in Serb-controlled parts of Croatia that had been operating in support of the Bosnian Serbs."[12] Moreover, when the Bosnian Serbs violated the safe areas by shelling *into* them, they were hit with NATO air strikes; but when the Bosnian Muslims violated the safe areas by shelling *from* them, they were only warned. It is no wonder that the Bosnian Serbs took UN troops hostage, because, in their eyes, the blue helmets were prisoners of war.[13] There is little doubt that the Bosnian Serbs were the aggressors in Bosnia, but perceptions about bias can be quite strong. For example, the International Criminal Tribunal for the Former Yugoslavia lacks legitimacy among many Bosnian Serbs because they have been the majority of the indicted defendants.

The Challenges in Peace-Maintenance

Subcontracting Complex Tasks

The authors of this book recognize that it is unlikely the UN, on its own, can assume all of the tasks required for peace-maintenance. One suggestion is for aspects of peace-maintenance to be subcontracted to regional arrangements. This option is provided for in Chapter VIII of the UN Charter and has already been attempted by a variety of bodies like NATO, the Association of Southeast Asian Nations (ASEAN), the Organization of American States (OAS), and the Economic Community of West African States (ECOWAS). Knight acknowledges the weaknesses in the security capability of many regional institutions, but insists that there can still be some form of collaboration or joint action between the UN and regional arrangements and agencies in underwriting peace-maintenance efforts. The idea of a joint administrative authority composed of the UN, the parties to the conflict, and interested member states is probably the strongest contribution generated by the logic of peace-maintenance.

Nevertheless, there are inherent dangers in subcontracting responsibilities that are neither clearly circumscribed nor regularly accounted for. Morphet reminds us that states are not to use the UN's powers of legitimation for ends contrary to the charter. Unfortunately, this commonly occurs, particularly when the UN subcontracts out enforcement action. The P-5 have been notorious for placing their own national interests ahead of the objectives of UN peace operations—such as the United States in Haiti, France in Rwanda, and Russia in the "near abroad."[14] Chopra explains that the Joint Control Commission in Moldova was not impartial and proved to be an effective means by which Russia could manipulate the parties to suit its interests. Coalition commanders often claim international legitimacy and approval for degrees of forceful action that were not, in fact, envisaged by the Security Council when it gave its initial authorization for the multinational intervention. The UN Secretary-General concluded that the use of P-5 states in UN peace operations can "create the impression amongst the parties that the operation is serving the policy objectives of the contributing Governments rather than the collective will of the United Nations as formulated by the Security Council. Such impressions inevitably undermine an operation's legitimacy and effectiveness."[15]

The potential for UN peace operations to be hijacked by member states in their own national interest is not limited to the P-5. Regional powers also have a direct stake in the outcome of local civil wars. Therefore, they tend to interfere to ensure that a "friendly" party takes control of the instruments of state or, conversely, to prevent a hostile party from doing so. William Durch and Barry Blechman commented that the "interjection of regional forces into a situation often interjects regional politics as well, which may make one or more domestic factions unwilling to accept" peacekeepers from neighboring countries.[16] In the past, regional powers have obstructed peace operations in internal conflicts in several ways: (1) by providing military or financial assistance to one or more of the belligerents; (2) by violating UN-authorized economic sanctions; and (3) by prohibiting the UN from using its territory for border patrols, bases, or refugee camps.[17] An obvious example of obstruction occurred when the Thai military aided and abetted the Khmer Rouge during UNTAC's mission.

Asserting Humanitarianism

Antonio Donini makes many valid and insightful observations regarding the changing nature of humanitarian assistance in the post–Cold War period. In particular, he outlines the distortions that now characterize humanitarian assistance, like the militarization of aid and the selfish political economy of charity. His chapter should be required reading for anyone concerned with international humanitarian assistance. However, I am assessing its merits solely according to the development of the peace-maintenance concept. From this perspective, Donini's contribution raises questions more than it supplies answers.

First, Donini argues that economic development should be a concurrent aspect of the peace-maintenance package. However, given the fact that resources are being diverted from development to relief, the question looms of where the money is going to come from. The world's money barrel is not bottomless, so what is spent on emergency aid naturally reduces what can be spent on development. Another alternative is to select certain failed states or regions for "mini–Marshall plans" and prioritize the rest. This idea of triage may be a practical idea, but it puts the UN in a very difficult moral dilemma.[18] How would the UN draft a set of criteria by which lucky countries could be chosen as the recipients of a long-term and costly economic rebuilding program? While acknowledging the current inconsistencies of engagement, Donini does not help identify the type of factors that might be included in such criteria for humanitarian intervention.

Second, Donini asserts that the weaker the state, the stronger the UN role is likely to be. He is effectively advocating a form of impaired sovereignty: states that cannot govern themselves become targets of intervention.[19] This type of thinking, which is shared by the other authors in this book, would greatly detract from, and delegitimize, the legal equality within the international system that helps underwrite peace-maintenance. Peace-maintenance would lose its moral authority if it operated only in weak states and ignored crises in more powerful ones.

Third, Donini contends that the cost of inaction will undoubtedly be much higher—spreading conflict and anarchy of "Kaplanesque proportions" will soon threaten the stability of the entrenched capitalist citadel.

This view is not without dispute. Many in North America believe that they "live in a fireproof house, far from inflammable materials."[20] What is the economic or security threat to the West presented by conflict and starvation in the Great Lakes region of Africa? If there is a threat, how can ordinary citizens in the West be persuaded of the fact? The answer has to be more than the emergence of a "vision."

Accepting External Authority

The success of peace-maintenance depends on its acceptance by the local population. This may seem like an obvious point, but it is often neglected by scholars. Fortunately, Clement Adibe's chapter on accepting external authority throws a cold dash of reality on the peace-maintenance concept. Adibe highlights four requirements that must be met if a local population is to accept an international authority: (1) the authority must meet the socioeconomic needs of individuals; (2) the authority must use coercion responsibly; (3) the authority must be legitimate; and (4) the authority must be palatable to societies that have not been socialized to accept a distant authority. Clearly, Adibe is not sanguine about the ability of the UN, or coalitions of member states, to effectively meet these requirements.

Another issue illustrates the substantial obstacles facing peace-maintenance efforts to convince local populations to accept an international authority. According to Adibe, the essence of peace-maintenance is to bring people back as rapidly as possible into any enduring framework for conflict resolution. However, who in the local population is capable of accepting external authority? Failed states have no functioning or legitimate government that can provide, or deny, consent to an external authority. Therefore, do you negotiate with the combatants or try to bypass them and go directly to the people? Peace-maintenance doctrine asserts that "the UN needs to counterbalance or even displace the oppressor or warlords."[21] Certainly, the de facto local authorities cannot be ignored. The Khmer Rouge, the Somali warlords, and the Bosnian Serbs were all major actors in their respective conflicts and were not without either power or supporters. Peace-maintenance would be a guaranteed failure if it attempted to exclude from the process the very groups that possess the means and the will to prevent the establishment of an international authority.

Financing Joint Operations

Peace-maintenance will be costly, but who is going to pay? The UN has had perennial trouble with its own bills, so how can it assume even more expensive ventures? The UN's financial difficulties stem from the unpaid dues of many member states. In particular, the United States owes the UN over a billion dollars. While the UN is attempting cost-cutting reforms

internally, it is unlikely to be able to balance its budget without some resti-
tution on its outstanding accounts. This being the case, the UN is in no position to expand activities like pursuing peace-maintenance until it gets its
own fiscal house in order.

Options exist that could finance peace-maintenance.[22] The solution
may be to blend the UN's peacekeeping, humanitarian, and development
budgets. This could create savings through greater efficiency. Another alternative may be to download the costs of peace-maintenance to regional
institutions, or a coalition of states. Donini says that assuming control of
a failed state's natural resources, like private sector nongovernmental organizations have been doing in Cambodia and Liberia, may result in the
local population paying the cost of restructuring their country. Perhaps
even an airline or currency tax might work. Unfortunately, there has yet to
be a detailed study that closely examines the financial aspects of peace-
maintenance. This must become a priority if peace-maintenance is to be
feasible.

Conclusion

Peace-maintenance is gradually becoming a more concrete concept. This
book provides a significant contribution to peace-maintenance by further
developing many of its key aspects. However, more work is needed before
peace-maintenance can become fully operational. In particular, its architects need to formulate strategies for overcoming the political, military,
and economic obstacles that currently prevent peace-maintenance from
being properly implemented. Specifically, there needs to be some careful
analysis regarding how it can be adequately financed. My aim in this con-
cluding chapter has been to aid in the doctrinal evolution of peace-maintenance. If the questions raised in these pages result in further research
projects that advance the goal of peace-maintenance, then this critique will
have succeeded. ⊕

Notes

Duane Bratt is lecturer in the Department of Economics and Political Science at Mount
Royal College, Calgary, Canada. He received his Ph.D. in political science in 1996
from the University of Alberta, Edmonton, with a dissertation entitled *Peacekeeping
and Internal Conflicts: The United Nations in Cambodia, Somalia, and Bosnia.*

1. An exception can be seen in the debate between Duane Bratt, "Rebuilding
Fractured Societies," and Jarat Chopra, "The Peace-Maintenance Response," *Security Dialogue* 28, no. 2 (June 1997): 173–189. For some of the correspondence
generated by this debate, see Riccardo Cappelli, "Peace-Maintenance is not the
Response," *Security Dialogue*, 28, no. 4 (December 1997): 509–510.

2. Jarat Chopra, "The space of peace-maintenance," *Political Geography* 15, no. 3/4 (March/April 1996): 335–357.

3. There is a large literature on improving UN peace operations, but the various recommendations have remained largely consistent—regardless of publication date. A brief sample includes: United States General Accounting Office, *United Nations Peacekeeping: Lessons Learned in Managing Recent Missions* (Washington, D.C.: United States Government Printing Office, December 1993); United Nations, Internal Oversight Services, "Final Report on the In-Depth Evaluation of Peace-Keeping Operations: Start-Up Phase," UN Doc. E/AC.51/1995/2 of 17 March 1995; and United Nations Department of Peacekeeping Operations, *Multidisciplinary Peacekeeping: Lessons From Recent Experience* (New York: United Nations Department of Public Information, 1997).

4. Timothy D. Mak, "The Case Against an International War Crimes Tribunal for the Former Yugoslavia," *International Peacekeeping*, 2, no. 4 (winter 1995): 555–556.

5. Ibid., p. 552.

6. For an examination of this issue with respect to Haiti, see Michael P. Scharf, "Swapping Amnesty for Peace: Was There a Duty to Prosecute International Crimes in Haiti?" *Texas International Law Journal* 31, no. 1 (winter 1996): 1–41.

7. For an examination of the UN Secretariat's military capability, see Duane Bratt, "Preparing Peacekeeping for the 21st Century: Improving the UN Secretariat's Institutional Capability," *Airman-Scholar*, 3, no. 2 (spring 1997): 4–11.

8. On the destruction of the ideals of international civil service through geographic respresentation at the cost of merit, see Thomas G. Weiss, *International Bureaucracy: An Analysis of the Operation of Functional and Global International Secretariats* (Lexington, Mass.: Lexington Books, 1975): 54–62.

9. Brian Urquhart, "For a UN Volunteer Military Force," *New York Review of Books*, 10 June 1993, pp. 3-4. Also see the responses to Urquhart's proposal in "A UN Volunteer Military Force—Four Views," *New York Review of Books*, 24 June 1993, pp. 58–59; and "A UN Volunteer Force—the Prospects," *New York Review of Books*, 31 June 1993, pp. 52-56.

10. Report of the Government of Canada, *Towards a Rapid Reaction Capability for the United Nations* (Ottawa: The Government of Canada, September 1995).

11. Adam Roberts, "Proposals for UN Standing Forces: History, Tasks and Obstacles," in David Cox and Albert Legault, eds., *UN Rapid Reaction Capabilities: Requirements and Prospects* (Cornwallis, Nova Scota: The Canadian Peacekeeping Press, 1995), pp. 60–63. Also see Stephen P. Kinloch, "Utopian or Pragmatic? A UN Permanent Military Volunteer Force," *International Peacekeeping* 3, no. 4 (Winter 1996): 166–190.

12. UN Doc. S/1995/444 of 30 May 1995.

13. For an excellent analysis of the hostage taking in Bosnia, see Michael Wesley, "Blue Berets or Blindfolds? Peacekeeping and the Hostage Effect," *International Peacekeeping* 2, no. 4 (winter 1995): 457–482.

14. See Terry Terriff and James F. Keeley, "The United Nations, Conflict Management and Spheres of Influence," *International Peacekeeping* 2, no. 4 (winter 1995): 510–535; and Duane Bratt, "Explaining Peacekeeping Performance: The UN in Internal Conflicts," *International Peacekeeping* 4, no. 3 (autumn 1997): 51–60.

15. Boutros Boutros-Ghali, "Supplement to an Agenda for Peace: Position Paper of the Secretary-General on the Occasion of the Fiftieth Anniversary of the United Nations," UN Doc. A/50/60, S/1995/1 of 3 January 1995, par. 41.

16. William J. Durch and Barry M. Blechman, *Keeping the Peace: The United Nations in the Emerging World Order* (Washington, D.C.: Henry L. Stimson Center, 1992), p. 16.

17. Bratt, "Explaining Peacekeeping Performance," pp. 60–62.

18. Thomas G. Weiss, "Triage: Humanitarian Intervention in the New Era," *World Policy Journal* 11, no. 1 (spring 1994): 59–68.

19. Compare Steven E. Goldman, "A Right of Intervention Based Upon Impaired Sovereignty," *World Politics* 156, no. 3 (winter 1994): 124–129. Goldman linked sovereignty with democracy, but Donini appears to be basing sovereignty on a state's governing capability.

20. This point was made by Canadian senator Raoul Dandurand to the League of Nations on 2 October 1924. It was cited and the concept updated in Joseph T. Jockel and Joel J. Sokolsky, "Dandurand revisited: rethinking Canada's defence policy in an unstable world," *International Journal* 48, no. 2 (spring 1993): 380–401.

21. Chopra, "The space of peace-maintenance," p. 339.

22. Compare, for instance, Ruben P. Mendez, "Financing the United Nations and the International Public Sector: Problems and Reform," *Global Governance* 3, no. 3 (September–December 1997): 295–304; Anthony McDermott, *United Nations Financing Problems and the New Generation of Peacekeeping and Peace Enforcement* (Providence, R.I.: Thomas J. Watson Jr. Institute for International Studies, 1994).

Acronyms

———— ⊕ ————

ACC	(UN) Administrative Committee on Coordination
ARRC	Allied Command Europe Rapid Reaction Corps
ASEAN	Association of Southeast Asian Nations
CIAV	International Support and Verification Commission (Nicaragua)
CIVPOL	(UN) Civilian Police
DPA	(UN) Department of Political Affairs
DPKO	(UN) Department of Peace-Keeping Operations
ECOMOG	ECOWAS Cease-fire Monitoring Group
ECOWAS	Econimic Community of West African States
FMLN	Farabundo Martí National Liberation Front
ICRC	International Committee of the Red Cross
IFOR	Implementation Force (former Yugoslavia)
JCC	Joint Control Commissions (former Soviet Union)
JMC	Joint Monitoring Commission (Namibia)
JMMC	Joint Military Monitoring Commission (Namibia)
LAS	League of Arab States
MINURSO	United Nations Mission for the Referendum in the Western Sahara
NATO	North Atlantic Treaty Organization
NGO	Non-Governmental Organization
OAS	Organization of American States
OAU	Organization of African Unity
O(C)SCE	Organization for (formerly Conference on) Security and Cooperation in Europe
ODA	(US) Overseas Development Assistance
OIC	Organization of the Islamic Conference
ONUC	United Nations Operation in the Congo
ONUCA	United Nations Observer Group in Central America
ONUMOZ	United Nations Operation in Mozambique
ONUSAL	United Nations Observer Mission in El Salvador
OOTW	Operations Other Than War
P-5	UN Security Council Permanent Members
PDK	Party of Democratic Kampuchea (Khmer Rouge)

POLISARIO	Popular Front for the Liberation of Saguia el-Hamra and of Rio de Oro
ROE	Rules of Engagement
RPF	Rwandan Patriotic Front
SNA	Somali National Alliance
SNC	Supreme National Council (Cambodia)
SNM	Somali National Movement
SOC	State of Cambodia
SPM	Somali Patriotic Movement
SRSG	Special Representative of the (UN) Secretary-General
SWAPO	South West Africa People's Organization
UNAVEM II	Second United Nations Angola Verification Mission
UNDP	United Nations Development Programme
UNEF	United Nations Emergency Force (the Sinai)
UNICEF	United Nations International Children's Emergency Fund
UNIKOM	United Nations Iraq-Kuwait Observation Mission
UNITA	National Union for the Total Independence of Angola
UNOMUR	United Nations Observer Mission Uganda-Rwanda
UNOSOM	United Nations Operation in Somalia
UNPREDEP	United Nations Preventive Deployment Force (Macedonia)
UNPROFOR	United Nations Protection Force (former Yugoslavia)
UNSF	United Nations Security Force (West Irian)
UNTAC	United Nations Transitional Authority in Cambodia
UNTAG	United Nations Transition Assistance Group (Namibia)
UNTEA	United Nations Temporary Executive Authority (West Irian)
URNG	Unidad Revolucionaria Nacional Guatemalteca
USC	United Somali Congress
WFP	World Food Programme

Index

Abkhazia, 13
ACC. *See* Administrative Committee
on Coordination
Action(s): anticipatory, 32; combined,
13; corrective, 51; creative, x;
enforcement, 30; external, x; failures
of, x, 107, 111; frameworks of, xi;
humanitarian, x; joint, 32, 129;
justification for, 21; legitimacy for,
23; political, x, 35, 92; preventive,
32; self-interested, 32; strategic, x;
timeliness of, 91
Adibe, Clement E., 3, 9, 33, 54, 68,
100, 107–120, 131
Administrative Committee on
Coordination, 92
Afghanistan, 31, 84, 90, 93
Ahmed, Refeeuddin, 13
Ahtisaari, Martti, 11, 47, 48
Aid: coordination of, 28; deregulated,
89; development, 1, 85, 86; emer-
gency, 84, 86, 130; external, 28;
humanitarian, ix, x, 15; international,
86; material, 15; militarization of,
130; privatization of, 87; state-to-
state, 90
Aideed, Mohammed Farah, 26, 27
Ajello, Aldo, 53
Akashi, Yasushi, 13
Allied Command Europe Rapid
Reaction Corps, 98
An Agenda for Peace (Boutros-Ghali),
2, 5, 20, 86, 109, 120*n28*
Anarchy, 6, 7, 8, 121*n49,* 130
Angola, 31, 55, 57, 124; elections in,
52; humanitarian aid in, 84; in Joint
Monitoring Commission, 11;
National Union for the Total
Independence of Angola in,
52; peacekeeping failure in,
6; United Nations Angola

Verification Mission in, 10, 43,
52–53
Annan, Kofi, 37, 112, 114
Anstee, Margaret, 52, 53
Arusha agreement, 24
ASEAN. *See* Asociation of Southeast
Asian Nations
Assistance, 14, 43, 97, 103
Association of Southeast Asian
Nations, 31, 129
Atlantic Charter (1942), 2
Authority: acceptance of, 3, 107–120,
112–117, 131; ambiguity of, 67;
arbitrary, 64; assumption of, 14;
charismatic, 29; civil, 102; conflicts
of, 108, 119*n9;* constitution of,
108–109; disintegration of, 27;
effects of, 113; establishment of, 3,
14, 34–35; external, 3, 23, 33,
107–120, 123, 131; granting, 23;
interim, 5; international, 10, 22, 23;
internationally mandated, 27, 28;
joint, 9, 14, 15; joint interim, 116,
117; juridical, 14; legitimacy of,
29–30, 47, 116–117, 131;
legitimate, 107; local, x, 14,
28, 34; mandate for, 34; moral,
124, 130; in peace-maintenance,
10–13, 19–38; political, x, 3, 7, 8,
10–13, 19–38, 41, 107–112;
politics as, 108–109; reconstitution
of, 8; relationships, 23; and
self-interest, 113–115; structures, 8,
29; survival of, 9; traditional, 29;
trust, 14, 42; of United Nations,
112–117; use of coercion in,
115–116

Baker, James, 7
Basic Principles on the Independence
of the Judiciary, 69, 72

"Bluespeak," 7, 22
Bosnia, ix, xi, 92, 98, 128; guarantees of movement in, 5; peacekeeping failure in, 20; relief operations in, 5; safe havens in, 31
Boutros-Ghali, Boutros, 2, 5, 6, 20, 120*n28*
Bratt, Duane, 3, 123–132
Burundi, 82

Cambodia, 2, 5, 31, 55, 57, 72, 90, 124; anarchy in, 6; civilian police in, 15; elections in, 14; interim authority in, 5; justice system in, 69; Khmer Rouge in, 50, 51, 64; lawlessness in, 66, 74; Party of Democratic Kampuchea in, 50; peacekeeping failure in, 6, 8, 9, 20; political institutions in, 9; rule of law in, 64–66; Supreme National Council in, 13, 50; United Nations Transitional Authority in Cambodia in, 43, 50–52, 64, 69, 74, 124, 130
Chad, 31
Chand, Prem, 11
Chopra, Jarat, ix, 1–17, 22, 24, 29, 35, 41, 42, 93, 107, 111, 117, 128
CIAV. *See* International Support and Verification Commission
CIVPOL. *See* Police, civilian
Clinton, Bill, 32
Code of Conduct for Law Enforcement Officials, 69, 73, 78*n31*
Cold War period: and civil administration, 43–46; effect of demise on United Nations, 19; peacekeeping operations in, 3
Colombia, 55
Colonialism, 9, 10, 93, 116, 117
Conflict: of authority, 108, 119*n9;* civil, ix, 57, 110; continuation of, 115; control of, 33; deescalation of, 27; internal, 2, 4, 7, 21, 34, 68, 88, 92; international, 19, 108; interstate, 21; intrastate, 21; legacy of, 93; prevention, 110; prosecution in, 63; regional, 31, 110; resolution, 5, 31, 33, 34, 107, 109, 110, 115, 128; social, 6; Third World, 110
Congo, 55, 93; Katanga secession, 44; United Nations operations in, 43–45
Control, 13–14, 43, 97, 103

Costa Rica, 31
Cousens, Richard P., 3, 15, 92, 97–104, 115, 126
Crocker, Chester A., ix–xi, 34, 56–57
Cuba, 31; in Joint Monitoring Commission, 11
Cyprus, 4; civilian police in, 15

Dallaire, Romeo, 24
Decisionmaking: effective, 35; international, 10; joint, 28; mechanisms for, 9, 22; ongoing, 25; in operations, 14; political, 8; processes, 35
Decolonization, 9, 11, 46
Development: aid, 1, 85, 86; emergencies, 93; of government structure, 14; long-term, 6; sustainable, 86
Diplomacy: interstate, 7; in peacekeeping, ix, 2, 3–6; and politics, 7, 111; preventive, 22; reliance on, 8
Dniester Republic, 12
Dominican Republic, 31
Donini, Antonio, 3, 9, 81–94, 102, 115, 130, 132

Economic Community of West African States, 31, 129
ECOWAS. *See* Economic Community of West African States
Elections, 53; conduct of, 5, 14, 21; as exit strategy, 14–15; incentives for, 52; international involvement in, 42; monitoring, 21, 42; organization of, 5, 28; planning, 51, 53; supervision of, 14, 47
Esquipulas agreements, 31
Ethnicity, 6, 21
European Union, 31
Evans, Gareth, 67
Executive Outcomes, 89, 90, 93

Factionalism, 6, 7, 8
Farabundo Martí National Liberation Front, 53
FMLN. *See* Farabundo Martí National Liberation Front
Fragmentation, 21

Genocide, 21, 25, 62, 63, 82

Globalization, 21
Gore, Al, 95*n7*
Government: legitimate, 34; rule of, 23; structures of, 93
Governorship, x, 43, 97, 103
Group of Friends of the Guatemalan Peace Process, 55, 56
Guatemala, 55, 57
Gurkha Security Guards, 89

Haiti, 31, 129; lawlessness in, 66
Honduras, 31
Humanitarian aid, 33, 66; as business, 88; militarization of, 83–84; protection of, 5, 22, 27, 82–84; as weapon, 1, 88
Humanitarianism, 3; assertion of, 130–131; and capitalism, 87–91; changing nature of, 90; geopolitics of, 81–87; in international relations, 83; in peace-maintenance, 81–94; redefining, 91
Hun Sen, 66, 124

IFOR. *See* Implementation Force
Implementation Force in Bosnia, 12, 13
India, 4
Indonesia, 45, 46
Information: campaigns, 46; control of, 45; dissemination, 46; management, 41, 54; objective, 47; provision of, 124; public, 46, 48
Infrastructure: damaged, 21, 33; destruction, 25; legal, 65; rehabilitation of, 5, 28, 33
Institutions: coalescence of, 8; collapse of, 21; emergencies of, 93; failure of, ix, 25; political, 9, 108; post-World War II, 20; reform of, 65; resuscitation of, 33; state, ix, 21; strengthening, 6
International Committee of the Red Cross, 87; internationalization of, 95*n2*
International Covenant on Civil and Political Rights (1966), 69, 71–72
Internationalism, ix
International Law Commission, 69, 70
International Support and Verification Commission, 31
International Criminal Tribunal for the

Former Yugoslavia, 70, 128
Intervention: criteria for, 83; external, 109; humanitarian, ix, x, 83; inconsistency of, 84; in interstate relations, 8; limited, 98; military, 2; multilateral, ix, x, 83; neutral, x; and prolongation of conflict, 84
Iran, 31
Iraq, 5, 31; aggression in Kuwait, 10; guarantees of movement in, 5; relief operations in, 5
Israel, 4

JCC. *See* Joint Control Commission
JMC. *See* Joint Monitoring Commission
JMMC. *See* Joint Military Monitoring Commission
Joint Control Commission, 12, 129
Joint Military Monitoring Commission, 11
Joint Monitoring Commission, 11
Justice system, 66; detention and imprisonment, 73–74; justice packages for, 67–76, 115, 124, 125; reestablishment of, 67; security for, 74–75

Kasa-Vubu, Joseph, 44
Kashmir, 4
Kenya, 85
Khmer Rouge, 50, 51, 64
Kirby, Michael, 72
Kirkpatrick, Jeane, 111
Knight, W. Andy, 3, 10, 19–38, 55, 100, 116, 127, 129
Kuwait, 5, 10

LAS. *See* League of Arab States
Law and order, 15, 61–77; financial implications of, 76–77; reestablishment of, 3, 61–77, 124–126; requirements for, 66–68
Laws: criminal, 15, 16, 69–70, 125; discriminatory, 47; elements of, 15; enforcing, 15, 27; humanitarian, 29, 89; prosecution of, 15; restrictive, 47; rule of, 15; sources of, 108
League of Arab States, 30
League of Nations, 3, 112
Lebanon, 4; warlordism in, 6

Lebed, Aleksandr, 12
Legitimacy, 118; achievement of,
    56–57; of authority, 47, 116–117,
    131; establishing, 47; for
    organization's action, 23; political, x,
    10, 41, 42, 54, 56–57, 127; politics
    of, x; sources of, 29–30, 34;
    sufficiency of, 52
Liberia, 31, 90; humanitarian aid in,
    84
Loi, Bruno, 115

Macedonia, 5
Mandela, Nelson, 31
Mexico, 55
Military: campaign planning in,
    101–102; civilianization of, 71;
    command tasks, 100; intervention, 2;
    multinational forces, 15; protection
    from, 21; relations with civil
    authority, 102–103; sanctions, 4;
    security, x, 3, 97–104, 126–128;
    symbolic deployment of, 3
Military operations, ix; demobilization,
    21; impartiality in, 4, 24, 128;
    internal conflict resolution measures,
    5; multinational, 4; observer
    missions, 4; political objectives in, 7;
    preventive deployment, 5, 21;
    reconnaissance, 24; self-defense in,
    4, 6; weapons confiscation, 21
MINURSO. *See* United Nations
    Mission for the Referendum in
    Western Sahara
Mohammed, Ali Mahdi, 27
Moldova, 129; Joint Control
    Commission in, 12, 129
Montgomery, Bernard, 99
Morocco, 8, 9
Morphet, Sally, 3, 14, 23, 41–58, 116,
    124, 129
Mozambique, xi, 5, 31, 89, 93, 124; aid
    to, 84–85; elections in, 52–53;
    privatization in, 85; United Nations
    Operation in Mozambique in, 43,
    52–53
Multilateralism, ix

Nagorno-Karabakh, 12, 13
Namibia, xi, 4, 55, 57, 63, 124;
    authority in, 6; civilian police in, 15;
    elections in, 58*n1;* interim authority

in, 5; Joint Monitoring Commission
    in, 11; United Nations Transition
    Assistance Group in, 11, 42, 46–49
National Union for the Total
    Independence of Angola, 52
NATO. *See* North Atlantic Treaty
    Organization
Neocolonialism, 33, 36, 116, 123, 127
Neoimperialism, 33, 36, 123
Netherlands, 45, 46
"New Partnership Initiative," 95*n7*
Nicaragua, 31
North Atlantic Treaty Organization, x,
    31, 98, 128, 129
Norway, 55

OAS. *See* Organization of American
    States
OAU. *See* Organization of African
    Unity
ONUC. *See* United Nations Operation
    in the Congo
ONUCA. *See* United Nations Observer
    Group in Central America
ONUMOZ. *See* United Nations
    Operation in Mozambique
ONUSAL. *See* United Nations
    Observer Mission in El Salvador
Operations. *See also* Military
    operations; campaign planning,
    101–102; categories, 13–16; center
    of gravity in, xi, 8, 101; command
    and control in, 3, 4, 22, 36;
    committees, 103; concepts of design,
    101–102; contingency planning, 102;
    counterinsurgency, 98; criminal law
    in, 16; doctrinal elements, 101–102;
    effectiveness of, 10; financing,
    131–132; joint, 131–132; means of
    governance in, 15; military, ix;
    multinational, 20; other than war, 98;
    peace, 21–22, 36, 41, 61, 98,
    99–100; planning for, 37; political
    direction in, 9
Organization for Security and
    Cooperation in Europe, xi, 12, 30;
    Final Act (1975), 42
Organization of African Unity, 24, 30,
    31, 32, 49, 93
Organization of American States, 31,
    129
Organization of the Islamic

Conference, 30
Organization(s): of civil administration,
  41–58, 124; development, 86;
  judicial, 72; nongovernmental, 62,
  85, 87, 89; regional, 9, 11, 30, 31,
  32, 112, 129; security, 19, 35
OSCE. *See* Organization for Security
  and Cooperation in Europe

Pakistan, 4
Panama, 31
Paris Conference on Cambodia (1989),
  50, 51
Partnership, 14, 43, 97, 103
Party of Democratic Kampuchea, 50
Peace: agreements, 24; international,
  21, 30; operations, 21–22, 36, 41,
  61; political economy of, 91–92;
  processes, 53; threats to, 21;
  transitions to, 62
Peace-building, 6, 33, 123; postconflict, 6, 22; pre-conflict, 22
Peace-enforcement, ix, 12, 108, 123;
  and collective security, 2; military
  nature of, ix, 3–6
Peacekeeping, ix, 24, 108, 109, 123;
  civilian police in, 15; consent to, 4;
  defensive, 2, 5; diplomatic nature of,
  ix, 2, 3–6, 9; interstate, 2; and local
  consent, 42; regional, 32; traditional,
  3, 4, 19, 104; training for, 37
Peace-maintenance, 2; assistance in,
  14, 43, 97, 103; campaign planning
  in, 101–102; categories of, 97–98;
  cease-fires in, 27, 49, 62; civil
  administration in, 41–58, 124; civil-
  military operations in, 62;
  conceptualization of, 20–22; control
  category, 13–14, 43, 97, 103;
  coordination of components of,
  19–38; critique of, 123–132; as
  decolonization, 9, 10; defining, ix,
  1–17, 41; drawbacks to, 33–34;
  external authority in, 107–120; goals
  of, 7, 10; governorship in, 13, 43,
  97, 103; humanitarianism in, 62,
  81–94; immediate tasks of, 27–28;
  justice systems in, 66–76; law and
  order in, 61–77; local community in,
  9; logistical support in, 35; long-term
  tasks, 28–29; medium-term tasks in,
  28; military security in, 97–104,

126–128; need for, 20; need for
  translation services in, 46, 51;
  operational, 10–16, 99–100;
  partnership in, 14, 43, 97, 103;
  political, 6–10; political authority in,
  10–13, 19–38; political economy of,
  91–92; as political strategy, ix;
  politics of, 3, 123–126; rapid
  reaction capability in, 25, 27, 35, 98;
  requirements of, 54–58;
  subcontracting tasks in, 129–130;
  subsidiarity principle in, 30–33;
  technical assistance in, 44, 72;
  technical/political lessons in, 54–56;
  as teleological imperitive, 109–112;
  trusteeship arrangements in, 36, 42,
  112; as unified concept, 3, 16
Peace support, 6, 97, 98, 103
Plunkett, Mark, 3, 15, 55, 61–77, 115,
  124, 125
Police, 53; abuse by, 66; local, 28;
  training for, 69, 72, 125; United
  Nations forces, 15, 35
Police, civilian, 15, 47, 61, 125;
  cooperation with other justice personnel, 63; independence of, 72, 73
Policy: defense, 97, 98; foreign, 57,
  111; national, 35
POLISARIO. *See* Popular Front for the
  Liberation of Saguia el-Hamra and
  of Rio de Oro
Political: action, x, 35, 92; alliances, x;
  allocation of values in, 108;
  authority, x, 3, 7, 8, 10–13, 19–38,
  41, 107–112; commitment, xi;
  competition, 6; conditionality, 85,
  86; decisionmaking, 8, 109;
  economy, 91–92; empowerment, 34;
  institutions, 9, 108; legitimacy, x, 10,
  41, 42, 54, 56–57, 127; management,
  2; objectives, 7; opposition, 66;
  order, 6, 108; parties, 53; pluralism,
  42; processes, 7; regimes, 42; space,
  121*n49;* stability, 29; strategies, 16;
  structures, 52; systems, 109; will, x,
  10, 34
Politics: as authority, 108–109;
  defining, 23; and diplomacy, 7, 111;
  international, 109; of legitimacy, x;
  nation-state, 35, 119*n9;* of peace-
  maintenance, 3, 123–126
Popular Front for the Liberation of

Saguia el-Hamra and of Rio de Oro, 49
Power: balance of, 14; bases, 23, 26; civilianization of, 71; colonial, 10; control of, 23; juridical implications of, 14; and justice, 42; legitimate, 108; policing, 15; resources, ix

Reform: electoral, 53; institutional, 28, 37, 65; local, 71; pressure for, 57; United Nations, 37–38, 131–132
Refugees, 5, 22, 28, 47, 62, 81, 90
Regional organizations, 9, 11, 30, 31, 32, 112, 129
Resources: allocation of, 23; constraints on, x; critical mass of, xi; development, 85; diversion of, 85, 130; financial, 34; human, 34; legal, 75–76; power, ix; privatization of, 90; specialized, 70
Rights: equal, 29–30; human, 15, 16, 21, 27, 29, 42, 48, 50, 51, 53, 57, 62, 64, 66, 67, 70, 71, 74, 86, 91; legal, 65; of passage, 22; property, 45; to receive assistance, 81; of self-determination, 29–30, 42; women's, 91
Roosevelt, Franklin D., 2
Russia: operations in near-abroad, 12, 129; participation in Implementation Force in Bosnia, 13; peace-creation operations by, 11
Rwanda, ix, 31; external authority in, 23–25; humanitarian aid in, 1; lawlessness in, 66, 82; peacekeeping failure in, 20, 23–25; relief operations in, 5
Rwandan Patriotic Front, 24

Safe havens, 31, 62
El Salvador, 31, 57, 124; authority in, 6; elections in, 53–54; Farabundo Martí National Liberation Front in, 53; interim authority in, 5; peace-keeping failure in, 8; Supreme Electoral Tribunal in, 53; truth commissions in, 71; United Nations Observer Mission in El Salvador in, 43, 53–54
Sanderson, John, 50
Security: collective, 2; global, 19; internal, 28; military, x, 3, 97–104, 126–128; post-Cold War, 19; public, 51
Sierra Leone, 89, 90, 93
Sihanouk (Prince of Cambodia), 50
Siyad Barre, Mohammed, 25, 26, 27, 116
Slim, William, 99
Social: chaos, 25; compacts, 68; competition, 2; conflict, 6; dislocation, 32; dynamics, 68; inequalities, 53; regimes, 42; relationships, 23; values, 23
Socialization, 117, 131
Society: breakdown of, 83; civil, 5, 21, 28, 33, 41, 84, 87, 93; development of, 41; protection of, 21; resuscitation of, 21, 28, 33; role restructuring in, 23; values of, 23
Somalia, ix, 2, 31, 110, 115, 116; anarchy in, 6; elections in, 14; as failed state, 25–27; Habar Gidir in, 26; Hawiye in, 26; humanitarian aid in, 1, 84; justice system in, 69; lawlessness in, 66; Manifesto Group in, 26, 27; peacekeeping failure in, 5, 8, 9, 20; relief operations in, 5
Somali National Alliance, 26
Somali National Movement, 26
Somali Patriotic Movement, 26
South Africa, 31; in Joint Monitoring Commission, 11; truth commissions in, 71
South Ossetia, 12
South West Africa People's Organization, 48
Sovereignty, ix, 16, 20, 46, 83, 87, 123
Soviet Union, 11
Spain, 55
Standard Minimum Rules for the Treatment of Prisoners, 73
State: accountability, 10; authority structures in, 108; building, 33; failed, ix, 25–27, 34, 36, 61, 107, 108, 112, 116, 118; institutions, ix, 21; reconstitution of, 108; ruptured, 21; services, 28; sovereignty, 20
Structural adjustment, 92
Sudan, 84
"Supplement to An Agenda for Peace" (Boutros-Ghali), 5–6
Supranationalism, ix
SWAPO. *See* South West Africa People's Organization
Syria, 4

Tajikistan, 12
Tanzania, 93
Thailand, 66
Tribalism, 63

Uganda, 24, 103
UNAVEM. *See* United Nations Angola
Verification Mission
Unidad Revolucionaria Nacional
Guatemalteca, 56
UNIKOM. *See* United Nations Iraq-
Kuwait Observation Mission
UNITA. *See* National Union for the
Total Independence of Angola
United Nations: accountability in, 8;
Basic Principles on the Independence
of the Judiciary, 69, 72; Centre for
Human Rights, 72; Charter, 2, 5, 7,
21, 23, 29, 30, 36, 42, 109, 110, 118,
129; Civilian Operations, 44; Code
of Conduct for Law Enforcement
Officials, 69, 73, 78*n31;*
commissions of inquiry by, 71;
Consultative Committee on Program
and Operational Questions, 96*n18;*
contributions to, 36; Department of
Peace-Keeping Operations, 37;
Department of Political Affairs, 37;
Development Programme, 54;
downscaling operations, 112;
Emergency Force, 115; Field
Administration and Logistics
Division, 37; financial constraints,
112; General Assembly, 9, 19, 29,
34, 42, 46, 127; in Haiti, xi;
ineffective operations, 10;
International Children's Emergency
Fund, 43; International Covenant on
Civil and Political Rights (1966), 69,
71–72; International Criminal
Tribunal for the Former Yugoslavia,
70, 128; intervention management
by, x; limitations of, 9; links with
field operations, 19–38; Office for
Development Financing, 37–38;
organization of civil administrations
in operations, 41–58; reform in,
37–38, 111, 131–132; relief
agencies, 87–88, 95*n2;* Secretariat,
10, 19, 24, 37, 112; Security
Council, 1, 3, 4, 9, 10, 19, 24, 29,
30, 34, 42, 49, 52, 57, 70, 86, 109,
126, 128; specialized resources,

70–71; special prosecutions, 70;
Special Representative for Human
Rights, 72; Special Representatives,
11, 43, 47, 53, 55; Standard
Minimum Rules for the Treatment of
Prisoners, 73; Universal Declaration
of Human Rights (1948), 69; World
Food Programme, 86, 95*n2*
United Nations Angola Verification
Mission, 43, 52–53
United Nations Emergency Force,
17*n6,* 46, 115
United Nations Iraq-Kuwait
Observation Mission, 5
United Nations Mission for the
Referendum in Western Sahara, 42,
49
United Nations Observer Group in
Central America, 31
United Nations Observer Mission in El
Salvador, 43, 53–54
United Nations Observer Mission
Uganda-Rwanda, 24
United Nations Operation in
Mozambique, 43, 52–53
United Nations Operation in the
Congo, 42, 43–45, 110
United Nations Operation in Somalia,
107, 114, 116
United Nations Preventive Deployment
Force, 5
United Nations Protection Force, 107,
116
United Nations Security Force, 45–46
United Nations Temporary Executive
Authority, 42, 45–46
United Nations Transitional Authority
in Cambodia, 42, 50–52, 64, 69, 74,
124, 130
United Nations Transition Assistance
Group, 11, 42, 46–49
United Somali Congress, 26, 27
United States, 55; in Haiti, xi; in Joint
Monitoring Commission, 11; in
Kuwait, 10
Universal Declaration of Human Rights
(1948), 69
Unocal Corporation, 93
UNOMUR. *See* United Nations
Observer Mission Uganda-Rwanda
UNOSOM. *See* United Nations
Operation in Somalia
UNPREDEP. *See* United Nations

Preventive Deployment Force
UNPROFOR. *See* United Nations
Protection Force
UNSF. *See* United Nations Security
Force
UNTAC. *See* United Nations
Transitional Authority in
Cambodia
UNTAG. *See* United Nations
Transition Assistance Group
UNTEA. *See* United Nations
Temporary Executive Authority
U Thant, 44

Venezuela, 31, 55

War: as business, 90; civil, 1, 34, 46,
90, 123; deaths, 1; guerrilla, 21;
irregular, 21; privatization of, 88
Wardingly, Ali Mohamed, 26
Warlordism, ix, 6, 21, 63, 82, 88, 92,
113
Western Sahara, 31, 55, 57, 124;
peacekeeping failure in, 8, 9, 20;
United Nations Mission for the
Referendum in Western Sahara in,
42, 49–50
West Irian, 55; United Nations
operations in, 43, 45–46
World Food Programme, 86, 95*n*2
World Summit for Social Development,
95*n*7

Yeltsin, Boris, 12
Yugoslavia, 2, 31, 110; ethnicity in, 6;
lawlessness in, 66; peacekeeping
failure in, 6; United Nations
Protection Force in Yugoslavia in,
10, 107, 116

Zaire, 1, 82, 84, 93
Zambia, 85

About the Book

The results of more than fifty years of peace operations—ranging from diplomatic efforts to the use of military force in so-called peace-enforcement—have made it clear that a new international political capability is required to adequately manage internal conflicts. That capability, peace-maintenance, is introduced and explored in this seminal work.

Varying in degree of engagement between governorship, control, partnership, and assistance, peace-maintenance is conceived as an interim authority that, in conjunction with local populations, represents the exercise of political authority within nations by the international community as a whole. The authors at once debate the legitimacy and effectiveness of peace-maintenance and clearly explain the dimensions and requirements of successful operations. Theoretical doctrine and practical experience are integrated in chapters on establishing political authority, organizing civil administration, reestablishing law and order, asserting humanitarianism, providing military security, and local acceptance of external authority. The result is both a review of past missions and a dialogue about the current and future politics of peace-maintenance.

Jarat Chopra is research associate and lecturer in international law at the Thomas J. Watson Jr. Institute for International Studies, Brown University. He is also director of the institute's Project on Peace-Maintenance Operations.